THE
BUSYNESS
DELUSION

12 SECRETS TO DESIGNING A SMARTER BUSINESS FOR A BETTER LIFE

CHRIS GARDENER

Let's Tell Your Story
London

COPYRIGHT

Dedicated to those who want to make a difference, create an impact and leave a legacy so the world is better because they existed.

CONTENTS

TABLE OF FIGURES

ACKNOWLEDGEMENTS

I was watching a movie recently. With only six main characters, you'd think the list of credits would be short and sweet. I was wrong – practically an army of people were listed. Maybe there was some serious forfeit to be paid if a single name was missed, no matter how minor or tenuous their connection with the film.

By way of acknowledgement, it is instinctive to list anyone and everyone who has had an impact on my life. Friends, clients, colleagues and noticeable strangers have all left their mark. It is, however, both unrealistic to attempt to recognise every single contribution. It is with some discomfort at the risk of missing and offending someone who's not mentioned, that I offer sincere and heartfelt thanks to the following people.

I've had this book in my head for more than three years. After a number of false starts, it refused to budge from being just an idea. Then Trevor "ToeCracker" Crook (a wickedly smart individual with a questionable taste in footwear, but who has a razor-sharp commercial brain and a genius for harnessing the power of words) recommended I get in touch with Colette Mason.

"She'll get your book out of you," he promised. The fact that you're reading this proves he was right. Without Colette's guidance and experience – coupled with her, "I'm not going to let you delay this" approach – I'd still be ruminating and pontificating. She's a wonderful publisher and coach, and I feel lucky to have worked together on this project.

While Colette is brilliant at extracting ideas from my head, it's a completely separate skill to help develop and nurture those ideas in the first place. This is the realm of a coach and in Dax Moy I have a world-class coach.

Formerly in Special Operations in the military, Dax has an imposing physique. Let's cut to the chase – he's impressively huge. If he was approaching you along a dark alley, your "fight or flight" mode would come down firmly on the "get the hell out of here" option. And if he caught you, he'd hug you. Because he's like that. He needs the body of a Greek god so it's big enough to house the most enormous loving heart you could imagine. What you see is most certainly not what you get with Dax.

Add to those beautiful qualities his knowledge of neuroscience and biomechanics, a complete and unwavering belief in and care for you, and an unparalleled ability to help you be everything you can be, Dax has a clear, consistent and inspiring coaching ability. He is truth, joy and love. He has had a huge impact on my life and long may that continue.

A book is never just a question of putting words onto paper. It's never just the author's efforts. There's always a team involved. And I'd like to thank and acknowledge Greg Fidgeon for editing, Wayne Savage for creating the inside illustrations and Sammie Covington for cover design.

A book is just words on paper. It develops a life of its own when those words become ideas, inspirations and insights in readers' minds. It is an exciting and daunting moment for an author when a book is exposed to the first readers. I would like to acknowledge and share my gratitude to my "beta readers" for offering their time and critique to make this book stronger: Sam Francis, Jo Spencer, Owen Dear, Ben Molyneux, Trevor Black, Dan Sager, Ian Redding and Kate Prinsep.

It's easy to have ideas. They feel exciting, inspiring and full of possibility. It's not so easy to turn those ideas into a tangible reality. For the last few years I have been a member of a very special group of men, whose unwavering purpose is to ensure every one of us shows up in life as the best version of ourselves.

There's no honour in playing small; in giving up on ideas. It would have been easy (and tempting) to let the idea of this book lapse into another "could have but didn't" project. I would like to thank and acknowledge the love, support and tenacity of these men: Yaron Engler, Simon Crowe, Keith Banwaitt and Trevor Black.

As a parent, I realise we can never know how our kids will turn out or what path they'll follow. To my own parents, I hope this makes sense of the work I've been doing all these years. I'm not sure you'll be any clearer on what it is that I do, but here's the result of who you created. I very much hope this makes you proud. I love you both and thank you for your love and support at every moment.

The toughest situation I've faced was the diagnosis, illness progression and eventual death of my wife, Ruth. We shared two-thirds of our lives together and I am very much a better man for sharing that time and love. Nothing I could say here would do justice to you or our love and time together. I will simply say: I will always love you.

To Helen and John, Ruth's parents, you have provided consistent love and support, giving space where it was needed and being there when that was needed too. It's never "fair" or "right" when you lose a child. I can only admire and acknowledge your dignity and determination during and since those heart-breaking times.

And to my children, Sarah and Adam, I am so proud of you. Losing your mum at such a young age is the hardest thing you could face. To have reached the stage you are now, with the futures you both have ahead of you, I could not be more optimistic and proud. I love you both with all my heart.

Finally, to my partner Kate: You have the heart and the patience of a saint. I felt I'd won the lottery with my first lifelong relationship. Now I realise I've won it a second time. I can't imagine a more caring and generous person to share my life with. You bring out the best in me. We have a big contribution to make through Gift of a Future – I love you and am proud to stand with you to make our own mark together.

Oh, and I'd like to thank Alfie the cat for allowing us the use of his kitchen as a place to get my writing done.

FOREWORD

"Oh no! Not *another* 'business success' book that's going to rehash the other 100 I've already read!"

That's probably what you're thinking to yourself right now and, to be honest, it's understandable.

Very understandable!

Pretty much everywhere you look these days you'll find books with titles promising you that you can '10X your business', '*Explode* your client base', create 'irresistible offers', 'scale up', devise a 'turbo-turnaround', 'build to last' or 'build to sell', all promising business owners the equivalent of access to some kind of 'secret' for business success that only those in the 'inner circles' know but that you, dear reader, can access for £12.99 + shipping.

That's not to say that some of these books aren't truly well thought out, superbly written and that the intention on the part of the author isn't to deliver the promise made in the book's title. I'm not that cynical and, as an author myself, I know just how much hard work, heart and soul goes into crafting every page, every paragraph, every sentence and, indeed, every WORD that goes into a book.

For most authors it truly is a labour of love to take what's in their minds and in their hearts, put it on paper (or digital paper) and share that with the world yet in the excitement to share (and of course, to sell) what they've created. Sometimes the promises made on the covers of books set the reader up for disappointment, frustration and pissed-offed-ness (it's a real word!) when they realise 200 pages in, that they're being told to do what every other business book they've ever read has told them to do; find the hungry crowd, build a better funnel, create a superstar team, cut unnecessary expenses, ramp up your ads and deliver phenomenal after-care etc.

You know, all that 'stuff' that you've heard before a million times. All that stuff that you've tried yet which didn't make the impact promised or yield the results you most desired. All that stuff that seems to hold so much potential and promise and that seems to be working superbly for the author and the case studies they refer to in their books but which just seem to fall flat, fizzle out and fail when you apply them to *your* business despite all the time, effort, energy and money you put into making them work.

All *that* stuff.

With so many books on business already in print, it may seem to some that pretty much anything and everything that could be said about these creating, growing, scaling and profiting from your business has been said already and, in many ways that would be true.

These days, very little of what finds its way onto our bookshelves is of the uniquely original variety and, instead, tends to be the general rehash of ideas that that most of us have already become *very* familiar with and so one could arguably put forward the case that yet *another* book on these topics adds very little but more noise into an already noisy genre and more of a drain on the highly-valuable yet rapidly-diminishing time we have available for '*getting stuff done*' in our businesses.

Yet, there's also another case that could be made and that, with your permission, I'd like to make regarding the book you now hold in your hands; it's that whilst the general *information* available to business owners may seem to to stem from the same sources and share the same general principles and ideas, it's not always the information itself that contains the *real* value to the reader.

We live in an age where one can pretty much find out all the information they want on any topic with just a few clicks, taps and swipes of their mobile device while sitting in their favourite coffee shop, drinking their beverage of choice, checking their email *and* holding a conversation with the person next to them.

We live in an age where information is abundant, cheap or even completely free yet one could conclude that the fact that there's so *much* information available to us about any given moment on any given topic is the very *reason* that business owners and operators are struggling or, as I like to say they are 'drowning in information and yet thirsting for knowledge'.

If that sounds like you, like you're one of those who are drowning in information yet who still finds themselves confused, overwhelmed, frustrated and burned out from constantly trying to make the information and ideas of the all those business experts and gurus somehow fit into YOUR business model and that you know full well that you don't need more rehashed information about growing a business but rather, what you need is a means to translate that information into *implementation* then I'm sure that you'll love what my good friend Chris Gardener is about to share with you within the pages of this book.

You see, unlike so many other business authors, Chris has managed to cut through all of the surface and superficial 'stuff' that most people *think* it takes to grow a successful and thriving business and gone deep into addressing the the core, essential foundations of what *really* matters and what *really* works when it comes to creating a business that is fun, fulfilling *and* financially successful.

It's worth reading that again.

Because most businesses these days seem to have been built around checklists that are designed to 'optimise output' or to 'maximise profits' which is all well and good and, of course, we all want profitable businesses, right?

But sadly, this checklist and task-driven approach is often at the core of why so many business owners are so stressed, overwhelmed, frustrated, burned out and *feeling* like they're failing even though their financial statements may say differently.

In this book, Chris not only reminds business owners about the vast difference between becoming a slave to a task-led, goal-driven 'Busyness' that you work for and the fun, fulfilling and financially freeing experience of mastering a business that works for you, but he also delivers a principle-by-principle, step-by-step process for making it happen too.

Chris is that rare blend of individual who is able to see the big picture while being able to go deep into detail, who can maintain focus on the *effects* and results that a business owner most desires yet who can maintain clarity and connection with the deeper, essential and fundamental *causes* that need to be addressed too.

Chris not only understand business but, perhaps more importantly, he understands business owners... perhaps better than many of them know themselves.

That's why you won't find a within these pages a book filled with tasks designed simply to fill up pages and and make it *seem* like there's a lot of value when, in truth, they just add to the already busy and overwhelming lives that most business owners are already experiencing.

Every story, every question, every invitation to put pen to paper has been *very* well thought out and has great intention behind it, not least of which is to help the reader to create greater impact, have greater influence and, of course, generate greater income without having to spend any greater time in doing so.

I know this for a fact.

I was there while Chris was formulating, creating and codifying the philosophies, principles and practices that he's so passionate about sharing with you in the pages ahead. I saw the care, attention and love that went into each and every part of this simple, elegant and *very* powerful system you're about to be introduced to and know that this is far more than 'just a book' to Chris.

In fact, as the name suggests, Chris's goal is to help you to completely, totally and utterly change your relationship with your business so that it delivers what you always hoped it would way back when you first started it and before busyness took over your life.

And, in my humble opinion, there's no-one better to teach you how.

In every way that counts, Chris is a *master* implementer who has learned to take action on every area of his life in ways that most could only dream of.

Whether it be growing his own very successful business, acting as CFO for others or coaching yet others still to their own successes supporting and helping to grow a charity that educates girls and young women in Uganda, performing regularly in a folk band (and even recording an album along the way) or travelling to far-flung corners of the globe to experience new sights sounds, paradigms and perspectives, Chris is a wonderful, living, breathing example of someone who has 'done the work' required to escape the Busyness delusion trap that so many business owners fall into and instead, create, grow and profit from the fun, fulfilment and financial freedom that we all started our businesses for in the first place.

And, in every way that counts, that what The Busyness Delusion is *really* about.

It's about learning how to dream, design and demonstrate those things that make a *real* difference rather than get hypnotised, hurt and harmed by those that don't.

Within the pages of this book Chris does a wonderful job of sharing not just the concepts and ideas that so many before him have written about but the practical, roll-up-your-sleeves-and-take-action processes and practices that make the *real* difference.

As you'll soon come to learn, Chris believes that in very real terms that there's a structure, strategy and system for building the businesses most of us dreamed of when we first started out and that it's far simpler and straightforward than most people would believe.

Fortunately for you, within this very book, he's willing to tell you how.

I invite you to not only read the words but to engage fully in what you're about to learn from Chris and to, perhaps for the first time, make the implementation of what's shared your greatest priority rather than just skimming the pages for the information.

There are principles here that may seem too simple, too obvious or even too weird at first... but open yourself up to them and do the work anyway.

Because when you've followed all the steps, you've done all the work and you look back upon what you've created you will, perhaps for the first time ever, come to really LOVE your business.

And it'll come to love you back.

And wouldn't that be cool? :)

Dax Moy

Author Of The MAGIC Hundred
Founder Of The GuRu Project
Creator Of The MindMAP Coaching Institute
National Academy Of Best-Selling Authors 'Quilly' Recipient

INTRODUCTION

ABOUT ME

When I was eight years old, I wanted to be a maths teacher. I loved the way numbers worked and I completely loved the feeling of helping a friend reach an "aha!" moment as they realised the secret to understanding something that was previously impenetrable.

If you were to cut me through the middle like a stick of rock, you'd read the word "teacher". Approaching 50 years later it's still a thrill.

Despite this, I never did become a maths teacher.

When approaching the finishing line of my maths degree at university, I became fascinated not only with numbers, but with psychology and how the combination of these two subjects created opportunities to make money. The life of an impoverished student is an effective motivator to finding ways of making money.

The consensus of advice to the fledgling Chris was: "Get a professional qualification – you can always fall back on that." A compliant and capable student, I followed this well-intentioned guidance and joined one of the UK's top professional firms. I qualified as chartered accountant three years later and found myself as advisor to many small businesses.

They were trading in a wide variety of sectors; from products to services, manufacturing to technology, start-ups to second-generation. I could not have planned for such wide exposure so quickly into my career. I was very fortunate.

It became evident that each business owner believed their business to be unique. Yet, from my privileged and professional perspective, every business was essentially the same. The details were specific, but the principles were common. Finding a competitive position, deciding prices, controlling margins and cash flow, organising teams, generating leads, creating a strategy and direction; all these and more were principles to be followed regardless of the specific products or services offered.

"The details were specific; the principles were common"

This insight ignited my "teacher" core. What was transparent to me was invisible to my business owner clients at that time. The reason was understandable – it was because they were buried in the hustle and daily grind of running their operation.

I may have had the insight, but I lacked the courage to make my own break for independence. There's great comfort being supported in large, well-run commercial organisations. I charted a course for my career that combined my love of teaching, finance (by then my preferred application of my love of numbers) and psychology.

I found myself in training, coaching and mentoring roles, initially in professional services but later in large commercial industrial organisations. I worked with business leaders in the UK, France, Germany, Italy, Denmark, Spain, Saudi Arabia, Dubai, Egypt, Hong Kong and the USA. What I taught them about the application of hidden business principles they then reciprocated in teaching me cultural differences between such a wide array of international environments.

This was a wonderful education. However, if you've ever had the dream of setting up your own business then that spark never gets extinguished no matter how comfortable your career may seem.

As my young children were just about to start their own journey into school education, it was increasingly necessary to resolve the conflict between international business travel and happy and healthy family life. There was only one possible decision for me: family first. I did not want to miss out on my kids' school years. It was time to become master of my own destiny.

It had taken 15 years longer than I'd imagined, but at last the "be your own boss" trigger had been well and truly pulled.

My initial business turned out to be highly lucrative and afforded me the lifestyle that gave me the family time I craved. Everything was going swimmingly. My friends and family weren't surprised as this was "capable Chris" continuing his successful and apparently easy life.

To be fair, this is how it seemed to me, too. But I was wrong. It was an illusion.

A couple of years into my new business, we received the devastating news that my wife was suffering from an incurable brain tumour.

Having been together since our mid-teens, we'd already had a longer relationship than many marriages. We tried to keep this perspective – we'd been lucky, happy and, until that moment, healthy. We had two wonderful children, a comfortable home and supportive families. Yes it was devastating, but we would cope.

And so we did. I reduced the number of clients I was serving as my priority was to look after my wife and the kids. The business had done so well financially that reducing the workload was an available option. As you'll read later, this is one vivid illustration of why financial security is so critical.

As my wife's condition deteriorated, it robbed her of her ability to walk, talk and be independent. During the last two years of her life I was her 24-hour, full-time carer.

Of course, the situation was dreadful, painful and we wished it were different, yet those two years were also beautiful, intense, loving and special. It was a privileged and honour to have such an intense time together. True, deep love, even when words weren't available.

That she was able to remain at home until the end — surrounded by family, friends and love — is one of my proudest achievements. However, the children don't stop growing. And life needs to carry on.

During those months and years I'd had plenty of time for reflection. While I'd successfully transitioned from corporate employment to being my own boss, I realised I hadn't built a business. This was the delusion. If I reduced my client work, my income followed suit. That's not a business; it's a job in disguise.

As the widowed, single parent of two school-aged children, it wouldn't be smart to jump straight back in to a job in disguise. It was time to put into practice what I'd learned — what I'd been teaching — over so many years.

Thus, I co-founded Strategic Mentors, which specialises in guiding self-employed business owners through the process of achieving what's most important in life: financial security, freedom and fulfilment.

WHY I WROTE THIS BOOK

This time — right here, right now — is the most amazing time to be alive. Despite media and news coverage doing its best to convince us everything is doomed, in reality the opposite is true.

At no time in history have we lived longer. We've never been healthier or better educated. We can travel anywhere in the world in a matter of hours. It's never been easier to earn money. We have more entertainment possibilities than we could possibly have imagined. We have the world's information accessible from a device in our pocket. We can communicate directly with someone anywhere in the world instantly and for free.

We can set up an international business for pennies. No longer do we need to be the servants to landed gentry or factory owners. The world is ours. We can make it what we choose.

And yet many dreams wither on the vine. The hopes and expectations of a new business too often find their level in mediocrity. The possibility of freedom is frequently abandoned; deemed unrealistic against a desperate, never-ending, hamster-wheel hunt for "enough money".

This happens not through lack of ambition, but because of the instinct to follow the herd and to copy what everyone else is doing. Learning from others has been an effective strategy for the last 70,000 years so why should it be ineffective when applied to building a business?

When we wanted to learn how to prepare our own food, it made sense to learn from those who were good at hunting and cooking. In other words, we learned from those who were already achieving the results we wanted.

Curiously, in business we seem less discerning when choosing who to learn from. We copy the marketing tactics of competitors not because they're achieving the results we want, but rather because we can see what they're doing.

Unsurprisingly, when their tactics produce mediocre results so do our imitations.

So, despite this being the very best time to be alive, people with the courage and conviction to start their own enterprises end up missing amazing opportunities. And yet, when they do turn their businesses into successes, extraordinary things can happen.

A ripple effect builds. Relationships deepen. Families become more connected and more loving. Communities become more engaged and less distracted. The daily pressure to earn enough is released and a greater purpose starts to emerge.

Despite this being an amazing time to be alive there are still very real problems and challenges in the world. If they're going to be solved, they need attention and resources. Entrepreneurs are the people best placed to provide both. They have the energy, drive and determination to get things going and build momentum. They also have the resourcefulness to make things happen.

They don't wait for permission – no entrepreneur became successful waiting for permission. They think, decide and act. Problems get solved. The world gets better. An impact and legacy emerges.

This is what's possible when you have the right kind of business – one that empowers, liberates and inspires you.

This is what's possible when you have a 3Fs business and life. Where you have financial security, freedom and fulfilment.

The path to all 3Fs is open. This book gives you the map.

WHO THIS BOOK IS FOR

When I give talks to rooms full of self-employed business owners, I ask them how their business is going. The common response is:

"Great, busy!" I then ask them if "being busy" is what defines success.

They realise it's not, yet they don't have a better answer. This is where I introduce them to the real purpose: financial security, freedom and fulfilment. I then ask them: "Do you have these 3Fs already?"

There's a consistent pattern to the answers they offer: "I think I've got two of them, but I don't yet have financial security."

As you'll see in this book, most of these business owners don't even have the 2Fs they think they have. They think they're fulfilled because they can say, "I really enjoy my work." They think they have freedom because they believe it means they can take a day off if they want to.

As one of the characters reveals in the story that follows, freedom and fulfilment are far bigger than these shallow responses. What's more urgent, though, is to act on the first F: Financial security.

You'll learn why this F must come first and you'll learn exactly how to achieve it on your own terms.

This book is written for people who are doing nearly well enough, but who don't have security of regular and predictable income every month. The business may be at start-up stage or may have been going for a few years. The age isn't the issue; it's the ups and downs of irregular and insecure income.

This is also for those thinking of starting a business. Every single day, hundreds of people make a start at a new way of earning money and making a living. Most will dive in, believing the priority is to "take action". Sooner or later, they'll be just like all the other start-up dreamers – being too busy and without financial security.

So, whether you've had your business for a while or you're just about to start, if you want to have financial security without the busyness, you're in the right place. This book is specifically for you.

WHAT THIS BOOK COVERS

There are 12 principles to follow to transform a business from a daily grind of feast and famine through to having financial security without the busyness. This book sets out those 12 and explains how to put them into practice.

The principles are structured in a framework – the Thrive Framework – four quadrants to make it simple to understand, remember and implement all 12.

A business doesn't just happen on its own. It needs a leader, an owner, someone making decisions to move it forward.

Consequently, looking only at business strategy, tactics and techniques will miss the critical personal dimension. Commercial topics on their own can never be the only ingredients necessary to create a thriving business.

Therefore, the Thrive Framework explained in this book includes two quadrants specifically focusing on the person, the individual – the skills and characteristics and way of thinking required to grow and build a 3Fs business.

Many are tempted to ignore the personal quadrants as they require introspection and often uncover unresolved issues they'd rather sweep under the carpet. However, avoiding these personal quadrants inevitably leads down the path to demoralising results: a lack of financial security, higher levels of stress and, in extreme cases, relationship breakdowns.

It's worth being clear, the personal quadrants are essential. This book explains why and the necessary elements to put in place.

The second two quadrants deal with business principles, making the best use of resources and building essential momentum. They demonstrate the consequence of "diving in" too early when setting up and trying to build a business.

They provide the antidote to overwhelm and busyness. They create the very best opportunity for the 3Fs of financial security, freedom and fulfilment.

You'll learn what a life with all 3Fs looks like. Perhaps more importantly, you'll discover what life without all 3Fs feels like. It's not common to recognise the 3Fs impact and even more unusual to bring all three into business and your own life.

There is more to life than, "I quite enjoy my work".

It is not freedom when it's the lack of work that allows you to take a day off if you want to.

Uncertain financial income is not "just how it is" when you run your own business.

This book reveals this ground-breaking 3Fs approach, and makes it accessible and practical for all readers.

THE HEROES

For the last 70,000 years, humans have passed knowledge down the generations through stories. Before the invention of writing, before the advent of the printing press and way before the modern miracle of electronic publishing, stories were the most effective method of teaching and remembering the wisdom of elders.

I could have written this as a pure "how to" book to join the ranks of countless others; many of which may be gathering dust on your shelf already. I have plenty of such titles in my own library, which is how I recognise this reality.

There are a small handful of these books that I remember. They are the ones that had most impact on me. They are the books whose wisdom I most readily recall.

Although they cover very different topics, they all have one thing in common: they tell a story.

There is no courage in playing small. My intention is for this book to have such an impact on you, dear reader, that you are inspired and able to make breakthrough changes to your business, so that you create an extraordinary lifestyle.

If this is your first reading of this book, the chances are you have no idea what amazing possibilities are in front of you. You are yet to experience the benefits of financial security, freedom and fulfilment. My aim is to help you turn those possibilities into realities.

Through history, changes such as these weren't achieved by "telling you how to do it". Changes of this scale were set in motion through stories, which both inspired and explained the necessary actions to take.

Hence, it was clear to me that the best way to inform and inspire you was to tell you a story.

It's a story centred on two characters, Simon and Frank. They are the heroes of this book.

Although they are both fictional, they represent an amalgamation of characteristics, skills and personalities of a great many of the wonderful clients and friends I've known over the years.

You may recognise some of Simon's situation in your own. He has been trying to build his business for a few years, but has never yet replaced the healthy salary from his last job.

Frank was in the same situation many years previous. He cracked the code to make his business and his life worthy of being role models.

You'll see Frank help Simon to understand that his current struggle is not his fault, as well as teaching and guiding him through the principles that will transform his business and life.

Just as Frank encourages Simon to implement these principles, I invite you to bring them into your own business and life.

You will be the richer for it, in more ways than one.

HOW TO USE THIS BOOK

Read the book twice.

The first time, absorb the story. See the common ground between Simon's situation and your own. Listen to the way Frank teaches Simon and recognise how Simon struggles at first before truly understanding each principle. Watch how Simon puts each one into practice.

The second time through, skim to the highlighted boxes of tips and diagrams. These form the structure for you to implement yourself. These are the building blocks for your transformation.

Complete the tasks that Frank shows Simon yourself. Being blunt for dramatic effect: your life depends on this!

As soon as you can (although I know you're less likely to act on this) I encourage you to teach these principles to someone else. This will take your understanding to another, deeper and stronger level. When you're able to teach someone, you know you've deeply understood the lesson yourself.

So now I invite you to read the story. Be open to the insights Frank shares and start to bring them into your own life.

There's no other time than now.

RESOURCES

At various points in the story Frank gives Simon tasks, often backed up with specific tools to help him.

The same tools are available for you to use. You can get them from my website http://thebusynessdelusion.com.

You'll find each one conveniently listed in the resources section at the back of this book.

KEEP IN TOUCH

If you have questions, want to reach me or find out more about how I can help you solve this problem, then all the contact details are at the end of the book too.

LET'S GO

Now you're ready to read the story. You're about to experience the fly-on-the-wall sensation of a life-changing series of events.

If you're itching to dive in to sort out your business, first learn from Simon's mistakes. Learn why and how he made them.

Listen to what Frank has to share. It changes Simon's life. Maybe, it can change yours too.

Let me introduce...

PROLOGUE

SIMON

"Maybe I'm just not cut out to work for myself."

Simon ached as he sat up from the hunched position he'd found himself in. He didn't know how long he'd been sucked in by this project, but it was long enough for it to change from daylight to darkness without him noticing. He squinted at the laptop to check the time. The harsh brightness of the screen cast a shadow across the paperwork strewn on his desk. He rubbed his stiff neck and tried to focus again. The relentless blinking digital counter taunted him, revealing it was 6.52pm on this Friday evening. It was the end of yet another 60-hour week.

It had been three years since Simon had started his own IT support business. Back then, he was full of energy, excitement and the aiming for the dream of the great self-employed lifestyle. Reality sucked. Right now, the dream of having a thriving business was as far away as it had ever been. Money was tight and the hours were killing him. He couldn't remember the last time he'd had a restful night's sleep. The energy to keep going was fuelled by his clients' problems and the fear of being unable to pay his bills.

It used to be easier than this. Money used to be easier than this.

Before Simon made the decision to become self-employed he had worked in large corporations. He would later claim he'd been a corporate wage-slave. The main upside of working for a large company was the apparent financial security. In such organisations there was always a need for IT managers and Simon was comfortable playing out that role. He managed a team to provide support services to different departments across TR Industries plc.

It was never the most exciting job, but he liked the company and he secretly loved being able to afford the house, the car and the annual holiday because this made his family proud of him. It felt good. To his family, he knew he mattered.

He'd met Susan while they were at university together. At the time, his friends told him he was punching above his weight. They were surprised to see them together and couldn't understand what somebody as attractive and popular as Susan could see in a geek like Simon, who'd be perfectly happy watching Star Wars or reading sci-fi. In truth, Simon was as surprised as anyone, yet the relationship worked. Despite the cajoling from friends warning him to hurry up in case he lost her, it was six years before he proposed marriage. When asked about why it had taken so long, Simon used to joke: "It's a big decision. I wanted to be absolutely sure she's right one."

Five days after their second wedding anniversary, Susan gave birth to Ben. Again, confounding anyone who offered advice and experience, Simon and Susan found it natural to cope with Ben's first year. They slipped into time-tested roles – Susan proving to be a capable, patient and natural mother, and Simon being the wage-earning husband, doing just enough around the house to show Susan they were a team.

The roles and the arrangements suited them perfectly. Eighteen months after Ben was born, he was joined by his sister, Laura. True to expectations, Simon and Susan were living the comfortable, middle-management lifestyle of nice house, nice car, a holiday in the sun and two healthy children.

Simon's career progressed. Each year his technical skills helped him climb another rung on the corporate latter. Each year brought a small but welcome increase in salary. Not sufficient to change their world, but enough to keep him loyal to the company.

And he was loyal. He felt proud to work for TR Industries and liked working with most of his colleagues. Over the years, when asked how work was going, his stock reply was, "Not bad, thanks."

One of the aspects Simon most enjoyed was working with his boss, Tim. They had worked together for more than three years, understood each other well and trusted each other implicitly. Then, one Tuesday out of the blue, Tim left. There was no warning and no clear explanation from the company what had happened. It was a mystery, but it was obvious to Simon that it was not wise to ask questions.

Tim's departure was a trigger that changed everything.

He was replaced by Owen who was, in Simon's opinion, a slimy, fawning, ambitious young pretender, desperate to reach the senior management grade as quickly as possible. Simon took an instant disliking to him, which developed into a deep-seated disrespect for Owen's skills, practices and character.

What had been a "not too bad" existence in TR Industries became painful and stressful. Owen was demanding more and more of Simon's time and the pressure mounted. As weeks and months rolled on, Susan could see Simon's mood darkening. He had little energy at home anymore and was no longer helping Ben and Laura with their school homework. He was changing and not for the better.

But what to do about it? She confided in one of her school-gate-mum friends how stressful Simon was finding work. She learned that her friend's husband had been through the same experience eight years previously.

He had taken life into his own hands and started his own business providing project management consultancy. Susan broached the idea of getting the husbands together in the hope that Simon could see a possibility for his own future.

The husband, Dave, was only too happy to share this wisdom and experience with Simon. He painted a rosy picture of self-employment. Yes, there had been some challenges in the first few years, but now there was no way that he'd return to the corporate rat race. The contrast between Simon's current clashes with Owen and the story Dave was telling stirred something inside.

When Dave described the frustrations he was having with his IT systems, Simon's mind raced ahead. He could immediately see there are hundreds of people like Dave, each running their own business and each likely to have IT problems that they had no clue how to solve.

Simon would solve them. This was how he'd build a business. This was how he would escape from being a wage-slave.

As if the stars were aligned, a short while later Owen called Simon into his office with the news that he was instigating a departmental reorganisation. One consequence of this was Simon's job would no longer be required. Two options were on the table: voluntary redundancy or apply for a role in the newly reorganised department.

Without giving away his true emotions, Simon asked for time to discuss these options with Susan. Within a week and with her full support, Simon had six months of redundancy money in his bank account and a new sense of optimism. His IT solutions business was on the road.

He dived straight in. Charging by the hour, his prices made him very competitive. His enthusiasm was infectious and he started winning clients quicker than he expected. He gained testimonials and more work kept arriving. It was a lot of hustle and he was always busy, but it sure beat working for Owen.

Once the initial euphoria had waned, the business found a steady rhythm. It was hard graft and took a lot of energy. After 18 months, he had nearly managed to replace his salary at TR Industries. Frustratingly, he was working much longer weeks than he used to, but he was hanging in there.

But nearly replacing his previous salary wasn't enough. Month by month, the redundancy financial cushion was shrinking. He just needed to be earning more. He always seemed to be chasing leads that he didn't get paid for and was running out of time and energy.

He had only one answer: work harder and work longer hours.

He kept this up for another 18 months, but it was exhausting. Susan's support and patience were stretched to breaking point. They no longer had any quality time together as he was consumed with the pressures of the business. It was clear he was heading for a meltdown.

Financially, his business flipped between feast and famine. When leads came in and he was busy, things seemed fine. The money flowed in and clients were happy. But with his time consumed by serving his clients to earn an income, there was no time left to find the next clients to pay him the following month. His monthly income was erratic to say the least. He dreaded another lean month, yet he felt he couldn't talk to Susan about it, because he wanted to protect her from the stress. She'd supported him enough already.

A few lean weeks turned into a deeply unsettling few months. What should have been an upward trend was turning into a downward slide; his confidence and belief seeping down an invisible drain.

As the pressure mounted, he found himself admitting to himself, "This just isn't working. I've swapped one job for another bloody job, and a worse one at that. This isn't what I signed up for."

He felt like a failure. At least in the TR Industries bubble he believed he was respected, even if he could see that the titles and management grades were an internal political nonsense. But at least he had a regular monthly income coming in.

He reflected that this up-and-down financial picture wasn't what Susan signed up for either. They used to enjoy life, spending plenty of time together, sometimes with the kids and sometimes precious times just the two of them on their own. Looking back, they didn't seem to have a care in the world. Everything was secure and safe. He could see it wasn't the most exciting existence, but much more desirable than the current financial uncertainty. He couldn't remember the last time he'd seen Susan smile.

His next thought hit him like a hammer to the chest.

He was letting her down. She had supported him when he was arguing with Owen, and she'd encouraged him and backed his decision to set up the business. And her reward was a stressed-out husband who could never switch off and, apparently, couldn't earn enough to replace what they'd been used to. He was relying on her to do the parenting for both of them.

Surely Susan was sick of this. Maybe she was ashamed of him.

He looked at his situation. He'd nearly replaced his salary, but inconsistently. He nearly had enough clients, but not quite. He was nearly a good husband, but couldn't step up. He was nearly the father Ben and Laura needed, but he was letting them down.

Nearly. Not quite enough. Was this to be the story of his life? Something needed to change, but he was at a loss of what or how to start that change.

He needed someone's help. Three years ago, Susan had introduced him to Dave because she knew change was needed. He decided to broach the current situation with her again.

Susan listened. She was grateful he was opening up to her. Given his usual reticence to express his feelings, she recognised that this was a sign things were serious. She knew it couldn't go on like this for much longer.

She was supportive and suggested: "I know you hated your last boss, which is what made you start this business, but being self-employed just doesn't seem to be working out. What about just getting a job again, Simon? We'd have security again and probably get to see each other more than we have done in the last year. You'd have more time for the kids too."

There, she'd said it. He was a failure. Should he give it up and go back to being a wage-slave again?

His next reaction surprised him. He could not go back to being a wage-slave. He could not allow himself to be a failure. He could see others running successful small businesses, so it was clearly possible. He wasn't stupid. Surely he was smart enough to make it work?

He had got his business to its current state with no help, no guidance and no outside advice. He'd been trying to do everything on his own. He'd been dealing with any problems as best he could, but he could now see his best was not good enough.

He realised it was time for him to stop being so proud. It was time to admit he didn't know it all and to get help from someone who had seen all this before.

Susan spoke next. "What are you thinking?" she asked. "You've been staring into space for the last minute. Are you going to start looking for a job?"

He looked across at her with determination in his eyes. "Susan, I've made a decision. I'm nervous and I'm frustrated, but I feel very certain that this is a positive decision.

"If I go back into the corporate job market then the rest of our days will be boring. Having this business has shown me how much better life can be when we make our own decisions, stop asking for permission and stop living by others' rules.

"Yes, I've struggled to make it a success, but this doesn't mean I can't make it successful. What I need to do is get some help. Get some guidance. I want to find a mentor and I want to turn this business into what we both hoped it would be."

Susan could see the Simon she wanted was back. This certainty, this commitment and this desire to make everything better.

"Simon, I love you and I'm behind you. Promise me this: you will listen to the mentor you find. You will do whatever they suggest. You will trust them. You will be open to new ideas and you will commit to making this successful."

"Susan," he replied, "I honestly don't know what I've done to deserve you, but I am very sure that I don't. Yes, I promise you everything in your list. I have no idea why, but I have never been more certain of a decision in my life."

"That's no surprise," Susan winked. "It took you six years to be sure of the decision to marry me."

Despite all the anxiety building up to this moment, the mood was transformed in an instant. Pressure and uncertainty were replaced with determination and clarity.

Simon knew what he had to do. Find his mentor.

FRANK

"I'm off now Jackie, see you tomorrow!" Frank called to his receptionist as he headed out the door.

It was 2pm on Tuesday and Frank had finished for the day. The sun was shining and he was looking forward to getting some fresh air while taking his dog for a long walk. The ability to decide when to work and how to spend his time never stopped being a thrill. It was one of the very best aspects of owning a business. He'd worked hard to create this situation and it made him feel alive.

It wasn't always this smooth. Frank's early days in his own business had many similarities to Simon's situation. But a life "wake-up call" gave him a fresh perspective, which led to him making significant changes in the way his business worked.

After leaving university with a physics degree, he was recruited on a graduate development programme in a large company that sold technical cleaning equipment to customers all over the world. The development programme placed each new graduate in a different department every six months. Frank realised he'd get direct exposure to all areas of the business. His plan was to build a wide and deep bank of knowledge and experience, and then start his own business.

He had no idea what his business would be, but he knew he wanted to be the master of his own destiny. He saw the development programme as an accelerator to his future success.

As part of the scheme, he was allocated a mentor to guide his early years in the company. He was partnered with Guy, a senior finance manager at head office. They hit it off quickly and easily.

Guy was well respected in the business, having held various financial positions there for more than 12 years. He knew how the company worked and he knew who was who across the numerous management teams. He knew where the problems were. In short, he was the ideal mentor for Frank.

As Frank gained experience in different areas of the business, he could see – with Guy's guidance – how the business worked as an overall process, not just a collection of different departments focused on their own priorities.

He developed the understanding of how new product ideas, typically originating in the R&D department, were market tested. He learned how they developed the selling approach. He dived into the details of how these products were built and delivered to customers globally. It was drilled into him how the sale wasn't a sale until the money was in the bank.

He learned how the company ensured invoices were raised correctly and on time, and how they ensured collection of the amounts owed. He saw at first-hand how customer support impacted the success (or otherwise) of a product's launch.

Time seemed to have flown. Before he knew it, Frank was marking his fifth anniversary of starting with the company. Inevitably, after five years in the same organisation, he was becoming jaded with the internal politics and the slow pace of decision making. Thanks to the graduate development programme, and with Guy's insight, support and guidance, Frank had high confidence in his own abilities.

He felt it was time to jump from the safety net of a large employer to becoming a "big fish" in a smaller company. He relished the idea of having personal responsibility for a company's growth. He wanted to make his mark. He believed this opportunity would be years away if he stayed where he was. The grass was becoming greener in a smaller business.

Over several weeks he talked this idea through with his wife Jane. They'd met at university and, after two years of being together, decided to tie the knot. They were the first of their social circle to get married.

She had confidence in Frank's abilities and fully supported his plan.

It took him only two weeks to find his opportunity. He was recruited as operations director of a company employing 35 staff, which had been set up by the managing director, Neil.

The following three years took Frank's business education to another level. Removed from the safety cocoon of a large corporation, he quickly realised his knowledge limitations in a smaller company.

On the face of it, the company was doing well. It was growing, principally through the efforts of Neil, who was driven to make as much money as possible.

However, the reality inside the company was something else entirely. In his drive to grow sales, Neil was cutting corners in operations. Customer orders were often delayed.

Financial controls could not keep up with the pace Neil was forcing. Suppliers' bills were left unpaid as delays in collecting debts from customers created a cash squeeze. A number of those customers were delaying their payments as they were unhappy with the quality or timing of the deliveries.

The problems weren't only in operations – sales were also starting to slide. The previous rapid growth of the company was built on Neil spotting a need in the market. However, to continue the pace of growth, he decided to bring in more products to create what he considered to be a better overall offer.

The market thought otherwise.

Despite Neil's attempts to drive the company forwards, the market refused to bend to his will. Month by month, financial results slowed. Rapid growth became "reasonable" growth. Then reasonable growth became "some" growth. Eventually "any" growth slipped into "negative" growth.

Frank could see the writing on the wall. Although he'd turned around many of the operational problems, Neil wouldn't listen to his solutions to turn the sales problem around.

With the never-ending stress, and declining results, Frank could feel his own entrepreneurial urge reigniting. It felt like time to make his break.

Frank had realised the biggest factor to determine a company's success was being able to create a compelling offer for the market. With this in place, he'd experienced how smaller companies struggled to develop an effective marketing and sales method. His own experience had shown him that when people found marketing and selling difficult, the company was in trouble.

Jane had her own career in publishing. With this steady income behind them if needed, she supported Frank's desire and together they developed the idea for him to start a marketing agency.

The early days were, inevitably, a rollercoaster. He worked hard to get his name and his offer known. As months went by, he developed a steady influx of clients. He'd designed his offer so that each client would become a long-term client; working with a monthly retainer fee.

His business was building smoothly. It was in control. He was enjoying his work and his clients were getting impressive results. His reputation was growing and more clients were seeking him out.

Until "the event".

Completely out of the blue, Frank had a heart attack.

He'd shown no symptoms of any problem. Yes, he'd been working long hours, but since working for Neil he'd grown used to coping with a stressful workload.

He was in intensive care for seven days. The doctors saved his life, but the tests revealed his heart was seriously damaged. He was under medical orders to take things much easier. The instructions were unambiguous – on no account was he to go back to working in the way he'd been doing. Whether he wanted to or not, something had to change.

As his agency had grown, he'd started to take on staff. By the time of the heart attack, he was employing a team of seven.

But his situation forced him to face a tough reality. Despite people admiring what they thought was a successful business, he realised he was living under a delusion.

He could see now, he didn't have a business at all. What he had instead was a job in disguise. In other words, if he stopped working – even with staff around him – the income would also stop. If he didn't work for long periods, he'd be in serious financial difficulties.

It was abundantly clear to Frank that to continue with a job in disguise was not going to be good for his heart and not a smart plan at all. Unwilling and unable to stop working, he used his recuperation time to redesign how his business must work in future. It was clear he needed to do less.

His new goal was simple – to create a business rather than a job in disguise. Unsurprisingly, Jane was strongly behind this intention too.

He set about the team reorganisation; changing who was responsible for what. As the team grew into their new roles, Frank invited their input to get strong and effective systems into the business. The combination of a more effective team and smooth and effective systems meant the company could scale up. Crucially, it could – and did – grow with Frank doing less. For the first time he was experiencing freedom from the business along with better income and working fewer hours.

His heart, his health and his marriage to Jane all benefited.

From his own growth, along with the same experience in most clients they worked with, he realised he'd tackled what he came to call the Busyness Delusion.

With the spare time he'd now created, he found himself exploring other ideas. Maybe there was more to life than building businesses.

Inspired by role models and speakers, he became interested in personal development work. This exposed him to ideas, practices and evidence completely outside his awareness thus far.

He learned about the power and impact of meditation. He studied aspects of neuroscience and was amazed how such knowledge could be used to for significant effect in business and in personal performance. He stopped taking his health for granted. From personal experience, it was clear to see how critical good health is and how everything else in life suffers when it is taken away.

His friends told him he seemed to be getting younger. Clearly, good health, good thinking, good business and a happy family came from a recipe worth nourishing.

He came to realise that, although he'd been helping people's businesses for approaching 20 years, he'd effectively been doing this with one arm tied behind his back. He'd been approaching these business challenges as one-dimensional: purely business issues.

What he'd learned through the personal development experiences was that any business challenge is two-dimensional: the combination of commercial business issues plus the impact of personal issues.

He developed this two-dimensional approach into a new framework and as he started using this with clients, their development and results accelerated.

This combined business-and-personal focus became the cornerstone for his professional practice.

One day, completely out of the blue, Frank's old university friend Simon got in touch and asked if he could pick his brains about business. Frank was aware that Simon had started an IT business a few years back. From what Simon said, Frank suspected he was experiencing the familiar pattern of the early years business start-up. He suspected the Busyness Delusion was in control.

Frank and Simon had always got on well, although they'd never been close friends. But if Simon needed help, Frank had the experience, skills and framework to put him on the right track.

He liked Simon and – as he always chose when and who to work with – he was happy to agree to meet, especially as Simon suggested they meet in the pub on a Friday night.

CHAPTER 1
THE REASON

As Frank reached out for the handle to the oak door of the Rose and Crown, he took off his hat and lifted his chin from behind his scarf.

He'd wrapped up and hunkered down into his coat to protect himself from the biting air. As he approached the pub, he lifted his head to see the warm and welcoming light from the windows set a stark contrast to the cloud-covered, black night sky. As he pushed the door open, the cold air gave way to the smell of wood burning in the grate and the comfortable sound of friends meeting up and sharing their stories from the previous week.

It was 7.30pm and Frank, right on time as always, scanned the bar looking for Simon. He was half expecting to be the first to arrive. He knew Simon was very busy and had learned that busy people are often late. So it was with some surprise he spotted Simon at a table in the corner already halfway through his first pint, hunched over his phone screen.

Frank navigated his way between bar stools and drinking buddies, shaking off his coat as he approached the table and smiling warmly. "Hi Simon. Good to see you here already."

Simon jumped up. He was clearly relieved to see Frank and anxious to get on with the conversation.

"Frank. Hello. It's good to see you. Thanks for coming. Can I get you a pint?"

With Frank's drink duly poured, Simon returned to the snug; placing the frothy pint on a fresh beer mat ready to soak up the inevitable spills from a busy Friday evening.

"That's a very welcome sight!" said Frank, taking his first taste. Wiping the froth from his lips, he looked at his friend.

"Simon, it's good to see you. It's been quite a while. What prompted you to get in touch?"

"Well, it's a bit uncomfortable to share this with you, to be honest," Simon said. "As you know, I've been running my IT business for a while now. The truth is that it hasn't lived up to my expectations. I'm at my wit's end. I don't know what to do next."

"Tell me more," Frank said.

"Well, I've been trying everything I can think of to make it work. As time goes on, though, it just gets harder and harder. I feel exhausted. I try to be positive, but the truth is that I feel stuck between a rock and a hard place. It's been affecting my marriage too. I mean, Susan has been more supportive than I could possibly have asked for, but she can see what this is doing to me. I snap at her and I lose patience with the kids.

"And now I've faced facts. Susan suggested I give up and look for a job again. That really shook me, I can tell you. But my reaction surprised me too. I realised that, even though the business isn't working at the moment, I absolutely do not want to go back and get a job. I need to make this work. And, swallowing my pride, I need to ask for help. That's why I asked to see you."

"It's a familiar story, Simon. Let's find out more. Tell me exactly what's happened and help me to understand the situation you're in." Frank leaned forward, set his elbows on the table and rested his chin in his palms, showing Simon he was fully focused.

"Well, the situation is that even though I set it up all full of optimism and I thought it would be really great after working for such a crappy boss at TR Industries, the truth is I don't have any time. I'm run ragged. I'm chasing new work, travelling everywhere to deliver the work I have got, and chasing people who haven't paid me.

"Not only do I have no time, I don't have the money to show for the work I am putting in. I'm not getting the rewards that all my efforts should have created. If I'm perfectly honest, I'm fed up with it. I was enthusiastic. I used to really enjoy this, but now it just feels like I'm on a hamster wheel going nowhere.

"I think if I was to be slightly dramatic about it, I'd say my life is going down the tubes. Apart from that, everything's fine. Everything is OK."

This didn't seem to be a surprise to Frank.

He sat back with a knowing look and said: "You know what your problem is, Simon? You're describing many of the symptoms of a contagious disease. Sadly, it's a condition that's afflicting the majority of businesses. I have evidence to show it's affecting more than 90 per cent of businesses in the UK alone, and the pattern is repeated in USA, Australia and most other western countries. It's an epidemic and no one seems to have noticed."

"What symptoms?"

"All those you described, Simon. No time. Not enough income. Not from a lack of effort. In fact, it's because of all that effort!"

"What is this disease?"

"I call it the Busyness Delusion."

"What's that?" asked Simon.

Frank looked Simon straight in the eye and said: "Let me ask you a question, Simon. Is the purpose of your business to keep you busy? Do you wake up every morning planning to be busy every waking moment of your day? Is its purpose to consume every thought you have during the day?"

"Of course not," said Simon.

"Well, no surprise," said Frank. "So, if the purpose of your business is not to keep you busy, what is the purpose?"

Simon looked blank for a moment. He'd never thought about it like that before. "I'm not really sure," he confessed.

"Let me guess what's happened," said Frank. He paused and reached into his case, pulled out a notepad and began to draw. He started by putting one long line down the middle of the page.

"OK, Simon. This line down the middle divides your life into two halves. On the left-hand side is your personal life and on the right-hand side your business life; your work and your career."

"Alright, yep, personal life, business life," muttered Simon, wondering where this was going.

Then Frank drew a horizontal line across the middle of the page, creating four quadrants.

"Here are two rows. The top row is for 'internal' matters. By this I mean the stuff you're thinking about. It's what's internal to your head. It's what's going on between your ears. And the bottom row is 'external'. This is everything else. In other words, it's what's visible in the world, not hidden inside your head."

"OK, I'm with you. So, this means you've got four boxes."

"Yes, exactly," Frank nodded, and then he labelled the bottom-left box with the word 'Reason'.

Figure 1: Thrive Framework structure

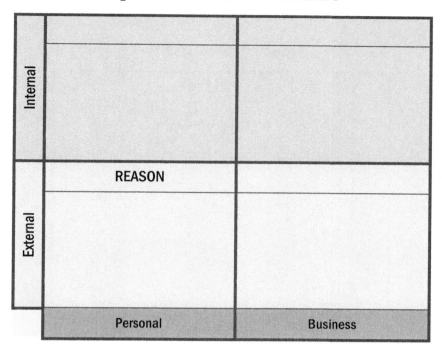

"This box is 'Personal-External'. In other words, it's what's going on in your personal life, outside your own head. This is a crucial box to understand, because this is where life happens. It's how you get to live.

"In fact, it's why life happens. Hence, it's called the Reason box. You started your business for a reason. I'm going to put my neck out here and say that the reason you went out on your own was because you found employment wasn't the Promised Land that you'd hoped for. You felt tied down, bound by corporate policies, affected by internal politics and probably surrounded by people you wouldn't choose to spend your time with. What you wanted was more freedom, more than just weekends and 24 days of annual leave and a company car. Does that sound right?"

"You must've been stalking me," said Simon, and he wondered where Frank was hiding his crystal ball.

Figure 2: Reason quadrant

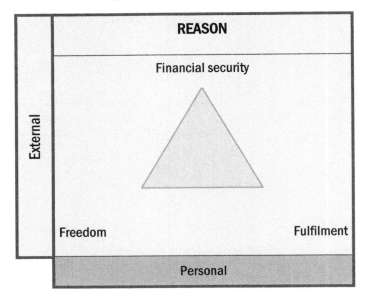

REASON QUADRANT: THE 3FS

"Here's my take on what a business is for," Frank said. "We have our businesses so we can have Financial Security, Freedom and Fulfilment. I call these the 3Fs. They come in a very specific order and I'm going to start with the third of the 3Fs – Fulfilment. Let's face it, what we all want from our businesses is fulfilment. Would you agree?"

"Sure," said Simon. "That makes sense."

FULFILMENT

"Most people's idea of fulfilment is fairly low level – it's a shallow idea," Frank explained. "They think being able to say, 'My job's not too bad' should be enough to be happy. They behave as if tolerating life is the same as loving life.

"To be fair, for most people, life nowadays is better than that of a medieval tanner who had the unfortunate job of curing cow hides by treading on them waist-deep in barrels of stale, week-old urine. So maybe it seems reasonable in this modern age for people to tell themselves, 'It's not too bad, it's OK-ish.'

"Now, when you start out a new career as a freelancer, taking a day off is OK. It actually feels great, because it's not possible when you're employed. The trouble is that you don't get paid for that day off like you do in a job. When you have more days like that over time, you naturally end up worrying about money. You're not really free to enjoy that free time.

"You become a prisoner inside your own head. You start to build up a sense of panic about the bills being paid instead of concentrating on the things you wanted to do, like enjoying your time with Susan and the kids without stress.

"Hence, with this perspective, fulfilment is something much deeper and more meaningful than, 'Things are not too bad. I quite enjoy my work'."

"I like the idea." Simon looked thoughtful. "But isn't being 'OK' more real? More practical?"

FRANK'S ECG IDEA

"Let me explain. Do you know what an ECG measures?"

"I think so," said Simon. "It's a measure of your heart rate, right?"

"Kind of," Frank replied. "It's not just your heart rate; it's how healthy your heart is too. I like to use the heart as a metaphor for what life is all about. If you've got a really healthy heart then, presumably, you're fully alive."

"I see what you mean," Simon nodded, becoming aware of the pressure he was feeling in his chest.

Frank went on.

"ECG formally stands for electrocardiogram, but in this context, I use ECG as a mnemonic of E, C, and G. These are the three dimensions that give us most fulfilment in life."

EXPERIENCES

"E stands for experiences. Experiences make you feel most alive. I've got a whole list of examples that I could go through with you, but I'll share two with you for now so that you get the idea.

"The first experience that makes life worth living is the experience of your love relationships."

"Well, right now, my marriage isn't in a very good place," Simon admitted. "I mean, don't get me wrong, I love Susan and, for some strange reason, I'm pretty sure she loves me. But she's put up with a lot since I've had the business. Or, I suppose more truthfully, she's put up with very little. I've been giving her very little. I've been so busy we haven't had time to be together like we used to."

"I understand," said Frank. "If it's any comfort, it's extremely common for people in your situation. And did you hear what you said? You said, 'I've been so busy.' I think we can safely diagnose you being yet another sufferer of the Busyness Delusion."

"But surely I need to be busy if the business is going to be successful?" Simon countered.

"Sort of," said Frank. "Being busy isn't a bad thing in itself; the delusion is thinking being busy is the answer to doing better. But we'll get to that. For now, I'm talking about fulfilment. Specifically, experiences and love relationships. Let's face it, if people are honest with themselves, love relationships are one of the most important aspects of anybody's life. When they're good everything feels great, but when they're below par, when there's anger or when there's disappointment, it's a terrible place to be."

"This sounds frighteningly familiar," said Simon. "It's because of Susan that I'm here talking with you."

"It's important, then, to make sure that your love relationships are really healthy and vibrant, would you agree?"

"Sure, of course I would. It makes total sense," said Simon. "But what's this go to do with business?"

"Isn't it because of the business problems that your own relationship has been stretched right now?"

"Yeah, you're right! I see what you mean." Simon's eyes widened as he thought about home life. "I just hope it hasn't reached breaking point."

"Love relationships are just one type of experience. Another type is adventures – what some people refer to as the bucket list. What do you really want to have done in your life when you look back on it down the road? Many people love the idea of having a bucket list. Not so many actually do something about it. What would you have on a bucket list?"

"Well, I know lots of people have amazing places they want to see or things they want to do," said Simon.

"Exactly," said Frank. "They want to travel to amazing places. Seeing the pyramids, swimming with dolphins, white water rafting, hiking the Grand Canyon, climbing in Nepal – wherever and whatever inspires them. They want to get involved in activities that they wouldn't normally do in life.

"So, Simon, when was the last time you did something like that with Susan and with your kids?"

Simon paused for a moment. "Well, I suppose I haven't done anything exotic since I left my last job. When I was employed we did go to the Caribbean, an all-inclusive holiday, although to be honest I didn't enjoy it too much. I was just recharging, just getting my energy back ready for my return to work. I didn't tell Susan that, though. I think if I was to look back on it, it was just going to the beach to just kill the time before I went back to work."

"So, that was how you were making the most of those 24 days of annual leave. Is that the picture you're painting?" asked Frank.

"Yeah, it was exactly like that. Now I think about it; that was no way to live."

"Exactly," said Frank. "It's like you were living on a treadmill. You were plodding along and, funnily enough, the faster you try to run, the faster the treadmill moves to keep you in the same place."

"Yeah, that seems like the right story,"

"Wouldn't it be better if you were able to live your life doing what you really wanted to be doing with the kind of love relationships that fill you up? Wouldn't your heart be fully alive and beating? Wouldn't an ECG paint a very healthy picture?"

"Yes," Simon acknowledged. "I'd never thought about it this way before. It seems like a dream, though. Is it reality?"

"Only if you make it reality, but that's entirely possible. It's my reality and I've helped many people make it theirs too. Maybe I can help you if this is the kind of life you'd want."

"Sounds intriguing," said Simon, wondering what Susan's reaction would be.

"OK, well hold that thought and I promise there is a way to build something that can give you that kind of fulfilment in life. But for now, do you see the point – that fulfilment means so much more than, 'I quite enjoy my work'?"

> **Frank's Tips 1** – Fulfilment is more than 'I quite enjoy my work'. Remember the principle of ECG – Experiences, Contribution and Growth.

"This is starting to really be an eye opener, Frank."

CONTRIBUTION

"Great. So, let me move onto the second part of ECG, which is the C. In this context it means contribution. Now, let me ask you another important question, Simon: If you were to look back on your life, do you think you've mattered?"

"Sorry," Simon looked uncertain. "Mattered?"

"Yes, mattered. For example, at some point in the future, when it's time for your funeral, do you think people are going to stand up and say, 'Simon was an amazing guy; he really mattered'?"

"Wow, this is getting pretty deep for a pub talk on a Friday night."

Frank looked calm. "Sure. We can go shallow if you like, but I thought you wanted to turn your life around."

Simon took a deep sigh, beginning to understand this wasn't going to be the kind of evening he was expecting. He decided to go all in.

"Yeah, you're absolutely right, Frank. If I was to think what would people say at my funeral, probably the best thing they could say right now is, 'He was quite good at his job and he wasn't a bad husband and father'."

"Right," said Frank. "If it makes you feel any better, you're far from alone in that. The reality is people just wander through their lives in their own little worlds focusing on themselves. If the best someone can say at your funeral is, 'I'll miss Simon. He was a great bloke and he doubled the size of his business,' you know you haven't lived a life that's really worth something.

"What does make a life worth living then, oh wise one?"

"What I've discovered is the secret to having a life that feels like you really mattered is to make a contribution."

"I'm not with you," said Simon.

"When you feel most alive you're not focused on yourself, you're focused on making life better for other people."

"Oh, right. You mean making a good life for Susan and the kids?"

"I'm sure you want to make a good life for them," said Frank. "But it could be more than that. It's entirely your choice. Some people find a great sense of fulfilment by making a contribution to their local community. For example, I know some people who are very involved in the church and they want to make a difference to the people who go to the church. For me, I wanted to set up a charity that's helping people in another part of the world and, I have to say, it's one of the most rewarding things that I could possibly have done with my life."

"Oh, I see," said Simon. "So, this is really quite big stuff."

"It's not about being big; it's about something that matters to you where you're helping someone else. The point is you're focusing on something beyond you. It's not all about you. You're making a contribution to other people and when you do that life feels pretty awesome."

"I think I can see what you mean," said Simon. "The trouble is, until I've got everything sorted it's difficult to really focus on making a contribution to other people."

"You're exactly right," said Frank. "What you've said there is more important than you realise.

GROWTH
"But, for now, I'm just going through the ECG part of fulfilment, which brings us nicely to the third element – the G, which stands for Growth."

Simon thought that, yet again, Frank was being cryptic. "Growth? Are we talking waistlines?"

Frank ignored Simon's interruption. "If you're genuine in wanting to turn your life around, we need to go a bit deep in this conversation."

"I'm intrigued and curious to go deep, but I was expecting to turn my business around, not my whole life"

"Turning your business round will be easier than you probably imagine. But you won't turn it around by simply implementing a magic bullet or a 'secret tactic'. That's the fallacy that seduces most self-employed people. The reason is that you don't have a business problem – you are the problem. Once you've set 'you' on the right path, the business follows naturally."

Frank's certainty and sincerity left Simon silent for a moment. "I don't have a business problem, you say?"

"You don't. You are the problem. This is true in every business. It's always the case. You'll see why as I explain more. Shall I go on?"

"Please do," Simon urged, genuinely meaning it.

"We've talked about death, but what about life? In order to be fully alive, the truth is that you have to keep growing, because when you stop growing you start withering and heading towards the end. I know that sounds doom and gloom, but it's true. You're at your best and you stay healthy and fully alive when you continue to grow. I think of growth in a number of different ways.

"One type of necessary growth is in your health and fitness. The reality is that if you haven't got good health and fitness then everything else in life plays second fiddle."

"I know exactly what you mean," said Simon. "Only last month I had a really heavy cold and I couldn't even function."

"Ah yes, man flu. It's terrible!" Frank replied. "That cold was a temporary blip, but think of all the people who are heavy drinkers or smokers. What are they doing to their health and how much vitality do you think they have in their future?"

Simon sheepishly looked over with a twinkle in his eye. "Fancy a second pint?"

"I'd love one," smiled Frank.

Simon headed off to the bar, grateful for a couple of minutes of calm to process the heavy discussion that he hadn't quite expected. He would learn later why he needed this break.

With two fresh pints poured, he re-joined Frank at their table.

"Cheers," said Frank.

"Cheers indeed and thanks for being here. It sounds like it's going to be a long night," said Simon.

"Maybe. We were talking about growth, right?" said Frank. "One necessary growth is health and fitness. Lose your health and you lose everything."

Simon knew what Frank had gone through when Jane was taken ill and passed away. He gave a knowing and reassuring nod.

"My kids rely only on me as their parent now," Frank added. "You can see why I take health so seriously.

"But let's move on to other areas of Growth – skills and knowledge and learning new things. It doesn't matter what it is, but when you're curious about the world and when you're fascinated about learning about a new subject, you can almost feel the growth happening within you. It becomes a fuel for your life. It doesn't matter whether you're talking about learning a new musical instrument, some creative skill like learning to draw or paint, or whether you're learning a new language. Even in your business when you're learning, for example, new marketing approaches..."

"I could really do with learning some new marketing approaches," Simon interrupted.

"For sure! That's to do with building momentum in your business," said Frank. "The point is when you're interested in learning, when you're pushing yourself forward and growing, you feel most alive and that all this is about reaching that deep sense of fulfilment I'm talking about."

"I think I'm starting to understand," said Simon. "It feels like the penny is dropping. I get the idea that if you've got no interest in stuff then, really, life feels like it's starting to end."

"That's exactly what I'm saying," said Frank. "I'm glad you're picking this up so easily. A final area of growth you might be interested in is what I call spiritual growth."

"You're not going to go all woo-woo on me, are you?" asked Simon.

"Not at all," chuckled Frank. "What I mean by spiritual growth is an inner resourcefulness. It's the place that you go to inside yourself when you need to dig in and have the resources to get through something that's challenging in your life. That could be how you actually go about growing this business of yours or how you make your relationship with Susan better. The more inner resources you have, the more capable you are of living the kind of life that's possible. If you lose the fire in your belly then you'll start to stall. Life feels less meaningful. It feels harder and it all starts to spiral out of control."

Simon nodded.

"So," said Frank. "Now you can understand why when I talk about fulfilment, the third F, it's so much more than, 'I sort of enjoy my job'."

"And yet," Simon continued. "If you asked most people if they're fulfilled, I think most would say something like, 'My job is OK'."

"A great life is a blend of experiences, contribution and growth, or ECG as I call it. You might be wondering how you make sure you're fulfilled. What did you do? You left your job to be fulfilled. Yet sitting here, halfway through your second pint, you look anything but fulfilled to me, Simon. You look knackered and out of shape. I get the sense that you're fed up, and you're clutching to that second pint because your inner resolve is weakened and you need to have some respite from the mess you're in. That's just me being Frank," he winked.

"This does sound important," said Simon. "But one thing is nagging at me: This is all very well and good having a deep sense of fulfilment, but the reality is I'm stressed to hell because I don't have enough money coming in."

"Of course you are," said Frank. "And I'm going to show you exactly how you can get enough money coming in and that's why fulfilment is the end result. But, before you can have fulfilment, you need to have the other things in place first, so that brings me to the second of the 3Fs, which is Freedom."

"Oh, I'd love some freedom," said Simon.

FREEDOM

"People think of freedom as meaning something like, 'I have freedom because I can take a day off if I feel like it'. That seems to be the sum total of people's aspirations when they have their own business."

"Well, I could take the day off if I feel like it," said Simon. "But that's more because I may not have enough work to do."

"Exactly," said Frank. "Being able to take a day off because you haven't got enough work does not mean you've got freedom. Now, as you're now getting the picture, I think of freedom in a fairly deep way. And I don't think of freedom as one aspect; I actually think it has six aspects."

"Six!" exclaimed Simon.

"Yes, six. Let me take you through them. The first one is probably no surprise. That's the freedom of time. It's being able to decide when to work. It's being able to decide when not to work. It's basically deciding how you want to spend or having the time to spend in the manner that you choose."

"Well, that sounds really desirable," said Simon. "But the truth is I haven't got any time freedom. I'm run ragged."

"I'm well aware of that. I'm getting the picture very clearly and we'll get that sorted," said Frank. "For now, the second type of freedom I want to talk about is the freedom of money."

"Freedom of money," sighed Simon. "I certainly seem to be free of money right now."

"That was me too. I got that T-shirt when I was starting out," Frank said, sensitive to what Simon was going through.

"This, of course, isn't freedom from money; it's the freedom to have as much money as you want. It's the freedom to never ever need to again say, 'I can't have this or I can't do that because I can't afford it'."

"Now that sounds like an amazing type of freedom to have," said Simon. "How on earth can I reach that level when I'm struggling so much already?"

"All in good time," said Frank. "We will absolutely get you there. But the third type of freedom is the freedom of client relationships."

"What do you mean?" said Simon.

"It's the freedom to choose who you want to work with."

"Oh my god, that would be amazing," said Simon. "The truth is right now, because I'm so short of money, I'm working with anybody who agrees to work with me, which feels like anyone who has a pulse."

"Right," said Frank. "I know there are some of those clients that you have who, in truth, you'd rather not be working with."

"Yep. There is a long list of frustrating customers I'd really like to kick into the long grass if I could. I get really wound up being forced to work with them to make ends meet. Well sort of meet." Simon's voice tailed off.

Frank continued: "Right, so being able to choose who you work with is one of the important freedoms that we want to aim for. The fourth type of freedom is the freedom of purpose. So, let me ask you Simon, what is the purpose of your business? What is the purpose of your life? Why are you doing what you're doing?"

"I really have no idea. You've really opened my mind to some big questions that feel important and yet it feels like you've created a great big vacuum," Simon said pensively. "The truth is; I'm not sure what my purpose is anymore. In a good week I've been a full-time geek but I've also been a part-time telephonist, a part-time tea boy, a part-time bookkeeper and, I hate to admit, a part-time husband and father."

"Yes, and that's why having a very clear idea of what your sense of purpose is really is so important," said Frank. "And that's why the freedom of purpose, the freedom to choose your purpose, is one of the freedoms I talk about. And then there's the freedom of location."

"You're not going to tell me about the laptop millionaire lifestyle, are you?" asked Simon.

"No, not at all. There are far too many scammers who are promoting that idea," acknowledged Frank. "What I mean by freedom of location is the freedom to choose where you want to be. The freedom to choose the environment that inspires you, that makes you feel good and that you enjoy being in. Tell me, do you have much to say about where you work right now?"

"Well, it's not exactly a glamorous office," admitted Simon.

"Tell me about it."

"I work at home and when I talk about the home office that's code for the kitchen table."

"Do you work anywhere else?" asked Frank.

"Well yeah, I'm always out fixing IT equipment at clients' bases and sometimes they can be quite a way away. A two-hour round trip for one job isn't much fun, especially if it's around rush hour."

"Right," said Frank. "So if you could have the freedom of choosing where to work, life would be better and you'd have more freedom, right?"

"Right," said Simon. "I see what you mean. God, there's a lot to think about here. I've been keeping my overheads as low as possible. I can't imagine paying for office space anywhere else at the moment, especially as the business is just me, but if I could work anywhere and choose only to work with people who were within striking distance then that would make a huge difference."

Frank smiled and continued. "And the final freedom I talk about is the freedom of health. As I mentioned earlier when we spoke about fulfilment, if you don't have good health you're going to struggle in whatever you try to do. It's the most important aspect of your life. Now, being Frank, I don't need to ask you too much about that I reckon. I can see the effects of your Friday night takeaway habit."

"Yeah, all right, I know where you're going with this," said Simon as he sucked his belly in and pushed his pint slightly further away from him.

"OK, so I think we can both agree that you're not currently in the full flush of youthful health, but do you understand why looking at life in this way and understanding all six of these types of freedom really matters?"

"Honestly, I've never thought about it like this before, but I can see that not thinking about it like this is having an incredibly high price on my life."

"I'm really glad to hear you say that because I think you're exactly right," said Frank.

> **Frank's Tips 2** – *Freedom* means more than, 'I can take a day off if I feel like it'. There are six types of freedom: Time, money, client relationships, purpose, location and health.

"Sure. Well, it absolutely all makes sense and I can see the importance of freedom, but again I come back to the point that the reason that I thought you might be able to help me is because I'm so stressed because I actually haven't got enough money."

"This is where the rubber hits the road," said Frank. "This brings us slap bang into the final one of my 3Fs, which is financial security."

"Oh boy, that sounds good. Tell me all about that," said Simon.

FINANCIAL SECURITY

"I'm talking about this last, but it actually comes before the other Fs. Again, the way most people think of financial security doesn't help. I like to think of it fairly simply. The way I define it is that financial security simply means breathing space. It doesn't mean wealth or months and months of saving behind you, it means that you have a financial breathing space."

"It's encouraging to hear I don't need big savings to have financial security," replied Simon. "Tell me more about it."

"Remember when you used to be able to go on those glamorous foreign holidays?"

"Oh, thanks very much," said Simon. "Rub salt into the wound why don't you! I thought you were supposed to be on my side."

"Well, yes. I'm winding you up, but there is a point to this," said Frank. "You remember those safety videos that they always show before take-off on the plane? How to put on the life jackets and where the emergency exits are?"

Simon nodded.

"Now, when they talk about the air pressure dropping what do they say?"

"They say the oxygen masks are going to drop down."

"Yes, they do," said Frank. "And then what do they tell you to do?"

"They tell you to put your own oxygen mask on first," said Simon.

"Spot on. Now why do they do that?"

"Well if you can't breathe you're not much use to anyone else," said Simon. "And I suppose it might take the edge of your holiday if you arrive in a body bag because you've suffocated on the way over."

"Graphically put, but you're right," said Frank. "If you can't breathe, nothing else matters. You can't focus on anything properly until you can breathe. People usually take breathing for granted. But they don't take it for granted when the air is running out because then it becomes really, really important. It becomes the most important thing in their life."

"Right, and what's the point that you're trying to make?"

"Well I like to say that money is like air. It's no big deal until you haven't got enough.

Frank's Tips 3 – *Financial Security* comes first because money is like air: it's no big deal until you haven't got enough.

Hence, financial security doesn't need to mean "wealthy", just to have enough monthly financial "breathing space" to remove immediate financial worry.

"You've got bills to pay. You have a sense of overwhelm that you can't cover those bills. Self-doubt kicks in and all of those start taking away the oxygen from your current situation. This is a problem because you didn't take the time to ensure you oxygen mask was firmly in place before you started doing other things.

"Before we start talking about freedom and fulfilment, we need to fix this bit first. We need to fix financial security. It's hard. When you're struggling and you're desperate for money and you're going out to sell your services, your customers and prospects sense that fear and desperation. They know when you are low on financial oxygen. They see you clutching at straws. As a consequence, it's not uncommon to end up working with people you consider to be idiots and the reason is that you're not able to take your time to find good clients.

"There's no time; you're just running around doing everything you can to find somebody 'with a pulse', as you said earlier. Anybody who's going to pay you money. As a result, you spend all your free time spinning your wheels trying to help them and win more of people like them as clients rather than gathering your composure, getting your act in gear and getting your own mask back on. If you can do that, that's where the proper solution comes."

"All right, all right!" Simon said, holding his hands up. "Stop it! Enough already. I can see you're describing exactly my situation. I can see the error that I'm making. Just tell me how to fix it."

"That's why I talk about financial security as the first F," said Frank. "It's the one that gives you breathing space in your business; it's the equivalent of putting your mask on. It frees up that brain of yours to sort your situation out."

"Sure," said Simon. "I can see that, but I still don't know how to get financial security or I would've done it already. I've tried learning stuff, I've tried one-day sales courses and they've been worse than useless. I've tried sending flyers out to people. I suppose they've probably become paper planes or gone straight into the bin. I've even read one of those 'book yourself solid' type of books, but I couldn't put any of it into practice. I found it a total waste of time."

"OK, listen," said Frank. "I don't normally do this but you've been my friend since university and I know I can help you. I know this because I've been through exactly what you're going through and I've cracked it myself. I don't want you struggling any more. Are you serious about wanting to change this?"

"Frank, I've never been more serious anything in my life," said Simon, earnestly.

"OK then. How about we start putting this into action on Monday morning?"

"Well, I'm supposed to be sending out a long list of marketing emails on Monday and making a few sales calls. You can imagine, I'm not looking forward to it, but needs must. I did say that I need to find more customers and more clients."

"Sure," said Frank. "Of course, sending out those speculative emails is such a priority because that approach has really worked with you up to now, hasn't it?"

Simon gritted his teeth, acknowledging the flaw in his own thinking. "OK, I can see I've painted myself into a corner. All right, screw the emails, Monday it is. I'll see you at your office. Thank you so much."

And with the seed of hope planted for Monday morning, Simon was happy to avoid talking about his problems for the rest of the evening.

They spent the next half-hour reminiscing about the times they shared at university and catching up on news of common friends. They parted company having finished their drinks. As Simon turned out of the pub and started his ten-minute walk home he was lost, deep in thought.

He had turned up to meet Frank hoping to learn some of the specific tactics that had made Frank's business so successful. Instead he'd learned some new terms: Busyness Delusion, 3Fs, ECG, six freedoms and breathing space.

Noting these related more to him than directly to his business, he sensed what was about to happen was much more significant than some tactical advice. He saw it would have a much longer-lasting effect on his life as well as his business.

He was reassured that Frank had said the first priority was the first F, financial security. This was exactly what he wanted to hear.

He had much to share with Susan and could feel the excited sense of hope rising in his body. He was looking forward to his Monday morning meeting with Frank. He was starting to believe his business was about to turn the corner.

He was ready.

CHAPTER 2
HEAD INSIDE

The sun was shining brightly on Monday morning. Simon saw this as a hopeful sign of things to come as he headed to Frank's office. He was keen to ensure that he wasn't late.

But, as he drove, he began to wonder what he'd agreed to. Susan had seemed encouraged by Simon's report of the meeting on Friday. However, now Monday was here and money was tight, he couldn't help but think those marketing emails he had planned to send weren't going to get done today. Although he was hopeful that this was going to be the start of a new stage of his business and a much brighter future, he felt his anxiety and uncertainty rising. He wondered if this was going to end up costing him. He needed his hope to override his nervousness.

He pulled up at Frank's office five minutes early.

The signs were positive. He was thrilled to find it was free parking outside the office and there was a space waiting for him. He walked up to the locked entrance and buzzed the intercom to be let in. As the receptionist greeted him, Simon couldn't help noticing a glorious smell of freshly percolating coffee filling the room. He could sense an air of efficient calmness, which was a welcome contrast to the niggles of the short car journey across town he'd just experienced.

Frank came through to the reception area and greeted Simon with a warm handshake. Heading down the corridor to Frank's office, Simon rubbed his hands together and said: "Let's get this business problem sorted. I need to get that financial security in my business."

Frank looked wryly to his side: "I love the enthusiasm and focus, Simon, but it's not quite as straightforward as all that."

The response left Simon feeling slightly deflated. They entered Frank's office and sat down on two sofas separated by a low table.

Frank had a sheet of paper already laid out. Simon could see it contained the same diagram they'd discussed on Friday. He could see the four quadrants and remembered the headings of the rows and columns.

"OK Simon, did you notice when we were in the pub that we didn't really talk about your business? I was interested in you, your life and how you felt about it. We were talking about what's going on with you and how fulfilment and freedom were working for you."

"Oh, course I remember," said Simon. "I've never had such a deep conversation in a pub on a Friday night."

"I'm not surprised to hear that," chuckled Frank.

"OK, so you remember the Thrive Framework I started drawing for you with the personal column and business column, yes?"

Simon sighed. "I wish I could turn that right-hand side into some sort of money-making machine."

"I know what you mean," said Frank. "There's more to this story.

"Remember how the top row represents everything that's going on inside your head, while the bottom row represents the results of all of that thinking? It's what other people see. It's what happens externally to your head. So, I call the top row 'internal' and the bottom row 'external'. Now, the bottom-left quadrant here is what we discussed on Friday. This is the Reason box. It's the external result of your personal column. In other words, it's what you want to happen in your world. It's how you want your personal life to be."

Now Frank drew a triangle in the bottom left square.

Figure 3: Reason quadrant

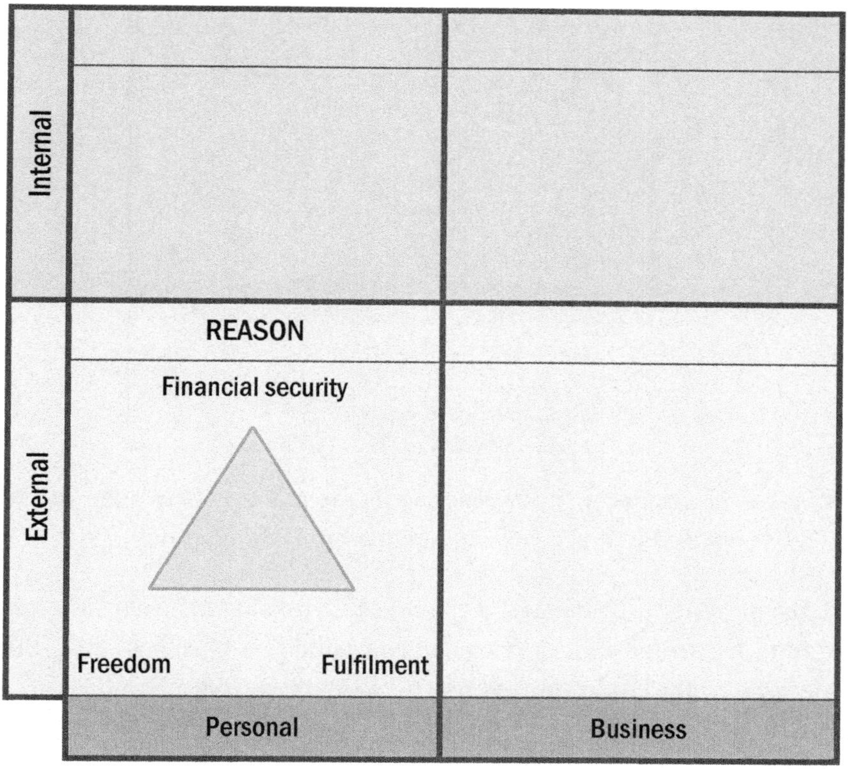

"Each of the points on this triangle represents one of the 3Fs: financial security, freedom and fulfilment. Remember the point I made on Friday? That they come in this sequence: You can't have freedom and fulfilment without financial security."

"Tell me about it," said Simon. "I've been trying to go on holiday but we haven't got the money!"

"OK, so this is the Reason quadrant," added Frank. "Staying in the personal column, let's now go inside your head. This is shown in the top-left quadrant. I call this the 'Self' box."

Figure 4: Self quadrant

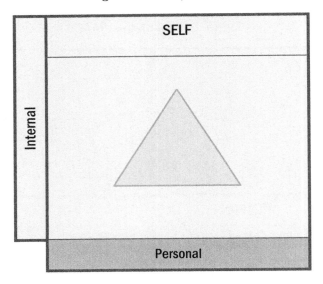

Simon was wondering if they were going to start getting 'deep' again. He just wanted to know how to make a bit more money.

Frank picked up on Simon's body language. He said: "I can sense you're getting frustrated that we're not diving into the business stuff. But there's a really important reason why we don't do that yet."

"Which is?" asked Simon.

"What you've done so far in your business, Simon, is what most people do as they start up. They dive straight in without thinking too much. You're saying you haven't got enough money. You've also told me you're working something like a 50 to 60-hour weeks right now. That's not far off double the hours you used to work in your last job.

"You've told me that you're spending about 15 hours doing IT support and about 40 hours of what sounds like fairly ad hoc marketing where you're worrying. You're flipping from one idea to another, pinning your hopes on nothing in particular and just hoping that by being busy enough you'll hit on some activity that pays off. But this approach is not bringing in enough new business. If you try to get more business just by being busier, you're going to end up working 80 to 90 hours a week.

"Then, when you're working longer hours for the same kind of results, what's the effect going to be on your relationship with Susan?"

Frank's Tips 4 – When you're already too busy at the current business level, winning more clients will only increase your busyness. Change how you attract and win more clients so it's easier. Or change what and how you deliver your solution to those clients so it's easier. Better still, do both.

Simon seemed to be in a trance. It was like Frank was reading his mind. He had been thinking he'd need to work longer hours to bring in more business. The way Frank described the inevitable impact of such an approach was a slap to his pride. The sudden mention of Susan's name snapped Simon fully alert.

"Woah! I hadn't thought about the impact on Susan in this," he said. "I was just focused on the money side of things and just needing more."

"I appreciate that," said Frank. "But there's more to your business than money, right? And Susan probably wouldn't be too happy with you working even longer hours. How much extra money do you think you'd bring in by working longer hours?"

"I shudder to think if I'm honest," said Simon.

"Exactly. What we need to do is find a new approach; a better way to be doing things."

"Right," said Simon. "You're talking about marketing in a better way."

"Well, quite possibly yes, but there's a lot to consider before we get to that stage."

"Really?" said Simon, seeing this would be no quick fix.

"Absolutely. There are many decisions you need to make that will make increasing your income much easier. But before we get to the business side of things, we have to understand why you have found it so difficult so far. And this takes us into the 'Self' box in the Thrive Framework. I'm going to draw another triangle in here as there are three elements to this area too."

"I'm starting to see a pattern," said Simon.

BRAIN

"The first of the points on the triangle is 'Brain'," said Frank.

Figure 5: Brain in the Self Quadrant

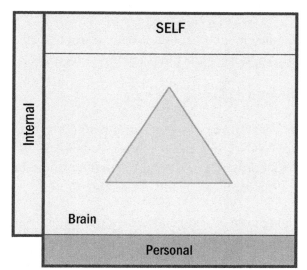

"Are you serious?" asked Simon. "You're going to start exploring my brain?"

"I'm totally serious and that may be surprising but you'll see why in a minute," replied Frank. "Would you agree that your brain controls everything you do? It controls your thoughts, your emotions, your actions and ultimately the results you get, right?"

"I guess it does, yes," Simon said.

"Right, and if you could control your brain better and understand what's going on inside do you think you'd end up with better results?"

"Yes, that's logical," said Simon. "But I'm already a good tech guy so what more do I need to know about to get better results? What's your point?"

"Here's the point," said Frank. "Here's a new way of looking at your brain and you'll see why it's so important. We'll be talking about a lot more than the bit you use to fix computer problems. And it starts with this: Your brain has one primary job."

"Just one?" Simon smirked.

"Yes, one primary job. Of course, it does a whole load more but it has one job that's more important than anything else."

"What's that?" asked Simon.

"Keep you alive." Frank paused for dramatic effect. "The fact you are sitting here shows your brain actually is doing its job really well. It is checking all around you all the time without you being aware. It's checking, 'Am I safe, am I safe, am I safe?'."

"I'm not sure my brain's asking if I'm safe right now," said Simon.

"Ah, you'd be surprised," said Frank. "Right now you're listening to me and concentrating on what I'm saying. But if you suddenly heard an explosion outside, do you think you'd still be listening to me and concentrating on what I'm saying? Of course not. Your head would spin around instinctively so you could look out of the window and see what's going on. That's because there's a part of your brain that suddenly got triggered and kicked into gear.

"There's biology at work here. As you know, we humans evolved over millions of years. The complex and brilliant brains we carry didn't suddenly explode into existence. Instead, our brains joined us on our own evolutionary journey. Our brains are built on the scaffolding of our evolutionary ancestors. In evolution terms, we have younger and older parts to our brains based on when each part came into being."

REPTILIAN BRAIN

"The part that gets triggered when there's a loud noise is the oldest part," Frank continued. "We call it the reptilian part of the brain."

"I've heard of that part," said Simon. "The reptilian brain is the part that does fight or flight, right?"

"Yes. Gold star!" said Frank. "And this part of the brain is ready for fight or flight when it detects there's potential for a life-or-death threat situation. When it's scanning and finds something it thinks might harm us, the reptilian brain gets active. It's that part of the brain that reacts when you hear the explosion."

"OK," said Simon. "But where's this going?"

"It's not very usual for our life to be in real danger," Frank added. "Yes, you may step off the kerb into oncoming traffic and then you're in physical danger – and when you do, you can be sure your reptilian brain will be firing off all kinds of signals. However, most of the time while you're fixing computers, there's no real life-threatening situation that you're facing, right?

"But your reptilian brain is still very much alive and very alert; looking for any opportunity to pop up and say hello. Hence it gets triggered even when it doesn't need to be triggered. When it's triggered, it floods your brain with 'watch out' chemicals and it is when you are in that state that you make decisions about your business. The impact on your business is not helpful. And the reptile isn't the only animal in your brain."

"How do you mean?"

"Further along the evolution journey, our brains developed as we became mammals. Hence we all still carry the mammalian part of the brain."

MAMMALIAN BRAIN

"Mammals were more advanced than reptiles. They evolved to work well together in a collaborative way. They formed packs and tribes and there was safety in numbers."

"Sure, this makes sense," said Simon. "But I'm still not sure where it's going."

"What's the worst thing that could happen to a mammal?" asked Frank.

Simon thought for a moment. "It would be a problem if the animal was left on its own without the support and protection from the pack."

"Exactly," said Frank. "That would be a life-threatening situation for that animal, right? And the brain, whose job it is to keep you alive, is very alert to that kind of danger; being sent away from the pack. Being isolated. Hence, to know that you're safe, this part of the brain needs social connection; it needs to fit in. And anything that gives the brain the sense you're going to be isolated starts to trigger an emotional response.

"You remember how the reptilian response floods the brain with chemicals that block out your ability to think rationally? The same is true of the mammalian reaction. This time it's not physical threat but social threat that turns the brain into an emotional melting pot. And when that's happening, we lose our ability to think, work things out and make good decisions."

"I think I see what you mean," said Simon. "You're saying that I shouldn't make decisions when I'm emotional."

"In part, yes. But I'm also explaining that we become emotional when we sense social threat. And that happens when we suspect we'll be judged. For example, like when we send out marketing materials or make a pitch to a potential new client."

"At just the moment when we want to be able to think and make good decisions," Simon realised.

HUMAN BRAIN

"That's how it affects you, yes. And where does the calm and rational thinking happen? It happens in the third part of the brain, which I refer to as the human brain. It's the youngest part of the brain in evolution terms. It's where executive function happens. It's where things like language, logic, music, creativity, art and problem-solving all get processed.

"It is, in essence, the part of the brain that makes us human. No other animal has the language capabilities, the logic capabilities or the planning capabilities that humans have. No other animal thinks, 'I wonder if I've got a one-hour time slot free next Wednesday afternoon?'"

"I'm sure you're right about that," Simon chirped.

"All your business problems need to be solved in your human brain," Frank continued. "You need to think logically, rationally and calmly to come up with the decisions and solutions that are going to turn around your financial position. But when your mammalian brain is triggered and your brain is flooded with chemicals that create an emotional response, it is practically impossible for your human brain to work in the way that you want it to work."

"OK. Let me see if I've got this right," said Simon. "Basically what you're saying is when I'm stressed I can't think clearly."

"Spot on," his friend replied with a smile. "Because this is how the brain works. So, while you're stressed and experiencing all the conditions that are creating an emotional response, it's almost impossible for you to come up with calm, logical and rational decisions and conclusions that are going to take your business to where you want it to get to.

"Before we get into being able to make business decisions, we need to make sure that you're calm and not stressed in order to find those solutions.

Frank's Tips 5 – Your brain has reptilian, mammalian and human parts. The answers to business and personal challenges are designed and created in the human brain.

The human brain can't operate effectively when the animals are in control. Increasing your awareness of your emotions starts to quieten the animals.

"So, tell me Simon, how do you feel about business right now?"

"Well, in the way you just described it, I'm stressed to hell. I've not got enough clients and yet the clients I do have want their problems fixed immediately. I'm trying to juggle time slots in my day. I'm trying to bring enough money in. I'm trying to win more work. I'm run ragged. So yes, it is pretty difficult to think clearly. But what can I do to get out of this situation?"

"You're picking this up quickly Simon. I'm glad. It's going to help you in a big way," said Frank. "The first thing I'd like you to do is to become more aware of what's actually going on in your day-to-day life and to do that I've got some technology to help you."

"Oh good. I like a bit of tech," said Simon.

"Yeah, I know you do and that's why I've gone for this new technology. It's called a paper notebook and pen."

"Are you kidding me?" Simon looked puzzled.

"No, I'm serious. Here's a notebook. And what I'd like you to do with this notebook is keep it with you for the next week and write down how you feel about what's happening in your life. Do this whenever the mood strikes you. What I'd like you to do is become more aware of what's going on inside of that noggin of yours."

"You're asking me to make a note of my emotional state whenever I feel like it?"

"Exactly," said Frank. "Because the more you become aware of your emotions when something happens, the more we can do something about controlling them. While your animal brains are in control, your human brain is left in the cold."

"OK, but it does sound a bit strange I have to admit," said Simon. "Are you saying this is going to make a real difference?"

"It will make a huge difference," confirmed Frank. "And that's not the only unusual thing I'm going to ask you to do now. As well as the notes, every morning I'd like you to take ten minutes for yourself."

"Ten minutes?" said Simon. "Sounds curious. What am I meant to be doing in those ten minutes?"

Frank looked Simon sincerely in the eyes and said: "I'd like you to meditate."

MEDITATION

Simon protested. He'd never meditated in his life. Wasn't it just some fad that successful people said they did, but probably didn't actually do? Why would they? What's it all about?

Puzzled, he looked to Frank for some further explanation and saw his friend was keen to do just that.

"What we need to do is to quieten your animal brains," he said. "We need to get back in control so that your human brain can come to the fore. One of the ways of quieting the animal brains is to become calmer and less emotionally reactive, and meditation is one of the most powerful and simplest ways to achieve that."

Simon paused to consider what Frank was saying. After a few moments he agreed to give it a go, although – if truth be told – he was doing it for Frank's sake rather than his own. "OK, but I have no idea how to meditate."

"Don't worry. There's a simple way to try it," said Frank. "I have a recording here that you can take away. It guides you step-by-step, so you'll be fine."

"Will I need to get a kaftan and a special cushion so I can sit in comfort in the lotus position to get in the zone?" Simon laughed.

"That is a common misconception about meditation," Frank countered, expecting the joke. "The type of meditation I'm talking about is one you can do anywhere. You can do it wherever you're comfortable at home or even parked up in your car. As long as you're comfortable and you can have ten minutes to yourself, anywhere is fine."

"OK. I'm in," said Simon. "And in the meantime, should I still carry on running around like a madman looking after my customers and trying to find more work?"

"Yes," Frank said. "That is what you need to do. Do the homework I've asked and continue working in your current way to win more work. We haven't changed anything directly in the business yet, so don't stop doing what you're doing to bring in the money that you so badly need."

"OK, I understand," said Simon. "I'm going to make some notes about how I'm feeling in this notebook and I'm going to try this meditation thing you've asked me to do."

"Good. I look forward to hearing how you get on. How about we meet same time next Monday?"

"Yes," said Simon. "I want to move on, so let's do that. I'll see you then."

They shook hands and Simon left the office and returned to his car. As he climbed into the driver's seat, he couldn't help reflect on another curious but intriguing conversation with Frank.

For the first time in ages, the first two hours of a Monday had flown by. He'd expected learn some business tricks that would help him win more clients. Instead he'd learned about reptile, mammal and human brains. He'd been given a notebook to capture his feelings so he could raise his awareness of how he was reacting in different situations. And to cap it all, he'd been asked to meditate for ten minutes each day.

The two conversations with Frank he'd had were sounding less like business advice and more like therapy. Yet he was beginning to understand why that mattered. The solutions to his business problems would be worked out calmly, rationally and logically. As an IT geek he felt comfortable with the idea of using reason and rational thought. He was going to enjoy rediscovering his human brain, he thought.

Then Simon realised that in the two hours they'd spent together, Frank had had no interruptions or crises to attend to.

"Lucky him," thought Simon. And he committed to himself that he would do what Frank had asked him for the week ahead.

CHAPTER 3
SMARTER, NOT HARDER

The following Monday, keen to do something about his fitness, Simon decided to leave the car at home and walk to Frank's office. During his journey, he noticed that he seemed to have a bit more space in his life. Maybe this was all down to capturing his emotions in the notebook Frank gave him. Maybe it was listening to that meditation recording. Who'd have thought it?

Simon also noticed a few other things on the journey to Frank's office. He noticed the car noise; the different tones that different vehicles made. For once he wasn't just listening to the whittling and worrying going inside his head. He realised that he did have time for trivia.

Along the way he also spotted a new business opening up and wondered if they might need computer help. He made a mental note to introduce himself to them after he'd seen Frank this morning.

He arrived at his friend's office, buzzed the front door and was let in by the receptionist. The coffee was once again percolating and smelt wonderful. Frank greeted him in the foyer and they repeated the walk down to his office.

"So, Simon," said Frank. "How was your journey today? Did you notice anything?"

"Funny you should ask," Simon replied. "I noticed a lot of potholes down the road and was wondering if they'd ever get filled in. But I'm being flippant."

"Interesting," said Frank. "I doubt they'll get filled in for a while. But you have noticed things going on, right? Things outside of your head rather than just the chatter going on inside?"

"Yes, you're right. In fact, I was thinking that only as I was walking here this morning."

"Great start," said Frank. "Let's get to that notebook of yours then and have a look through what you've written. Tell me something that didn't go to plan and what you noted about it. What did you realise?"

Simon flicked through the notebook, which was already looking surprisingly well used. "Ah here's one," he said. "Last Wednesday. I was out on a job and by the end of it I felt guilty that it took about three times as long as I thought it should. What I noted was I was frustrated about my slow performance. I felt guilty about charging the client for all three hours, because I actually misunderstood what the problem was. Then I noticed that my inner voice kicked in with, 'Here we go again; everything is so hard'.

"I was so wound up that I felt like just chucking it all in and finding a job. I remember now I'm reading this back, Wednesday afternoon felt like a write-off. I was just so fed up with this whole thing. I was totally demoralised. But you know what? I then noticed how that was an emotional reaction, just like you said. It wasn't a logical response and it certainly wasn't a considered response that I could use to solve the problem. Normally, I would have worked into the evening to make up for the lost time, but this time I decided not to. I downed tools and actually I took the evening off."

"This is great Simon, amazing," Frank replied. "You're starting to see the difference between the emotional reaction and a rational response. This means you're now starting to take control of your thinking. There's a way to go, but you're starting. You're calming the animals and being more human. Should we play with the human brain?"

"Does this mean we actually can look at the business problem now? Because, let's face it, if we're talking animals then the elephant in the room can't be ignored any longer. I can't live on fresh air and noticing car engines on a walk to your office."

RESOURCES

Frank chuckled. "Yes, OK," he said. "Time to get back to the Thrive Framework. When we looked at the framework before, you learned about the two columns for personal and business and we looked at the Reason quadrant with the 3Fs. I started to introduce you to the 'Self' quadrant, where we talked about the brain being one of the three points on the triangle."

"I remember it well," said Simon.

"OK. Well now I'm going to go to the top-right quadrant. This is what's going on inside your head in connection with the business directly. This is the 'Resources' box. Like the two quadrants we've already touched, this one also covers three principles." He added a triangle to this new quadrant.

"We haven't covered the other two principles in the 'Self' box yet," Simon pointed out. "That triangle only has one point covered so far."

"We'll come to those when the time is right," said Frank. "Let's get to the business column. You keep saying you want to solve the business problem."

MODEL

"Okay, so let's look at one of three elements in the 'Resources' box. This first one is 'Model'."

Figure 6: Model in resources quadrant

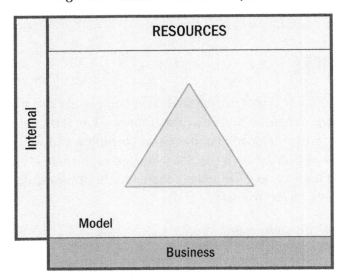

"What does that mean?"

"The Model is how you trade with your clients. What you offer, what price you charge and how often they buy from you. Interestingly, when most people start up their businesses they don't really think about this stuff. They just dive in and unwittingly create what is possibly the hardest model of all."

Frank's Tips 6 – Your Model describes how you trade with your clients. The decisions you make about your Model determine how easy or how hard it will be to meet your objectives.

"Hardest model? What would that be?" asked Simon.

CHARGING BY THE HOUR

Frank smiled at his friend and gave him the answer: "It's the one where you charge your customers or clients by the hour or by the day. You figure out all you need to do is to sell enough hours or enough days and you'll earn enough money to pay all your bills and have a bit left over."

"That's the most complicated model?" said Simon, puzzled.

"It's certainly the model that's needs hardest work," said Frank.

"Well it sounds like I fell straight into that trap hook, line, and sinker, right?"

As Simon winced, Frank grinned and asked another question: "Can you explain to me what you do for your customers now?"

Simon thought for a moment and said: "Well, they phone me the instant they have a systems crisis. They say things like, 'My laptop's dead', 'My printer has developed an attitude problem and refuses to print a single page', 'My customer database has disappeared', 'I've not had any emails for a week', 'My...'"

"OK, I get it. There are a lot of crises. Then what happens?"

"Well I tend to drop everything and go and see them and help them as soon as possible."

"Why do you drop everything?"

"What do you mean, 'Why drop everything?' That's what my business is! Who wants a slow solution to a problem?"

"Bear with me. Why do you drop everything there and then? Why do you rush to see them as soon as possible? What's really in it for you?"

"Their problem is right now and their stress levels are sky high. I build up a good reputation by being responsive to them and helping them out in their hour of need. I dash to their immediate rescue like Superman, I suppose.

"I might not have mentioned it, but I get most of my business at the moment through referrals and word of mouth. Happy customers mean more customers when they tell their friends. Plus, fixing the problem there and then helps me get cash quicker. Everything is hand-to-mouth at the moment, if I'm honest, and as soon as I smell a few quid, I'm drawn to it like a moth to a flame."

"And how much do you charge?"

"I settled on £45 an hour."

"So, you charge an hourly rate, right?"

"That's right."

"Do you charge the travel time to get there?"

"Well most jobs are local, so I don't normally charge for travel. But that over-running repair on Wednesday was actually an hour each way come to think of it. I didn't charge extra for the travel as I don't for other clients."

"I understand. You were being fair to all your clients. But let me ask, what was the price they were suffering while their systems were down? What was the consequence to them, until you sorted things out for them?"

"Funny you should ask, because they told me. Every hour their system was down was costing them about £2,500 in lost revenue."

"Interesting. Their systems were down for the hour you took to get there, plus the three hours on site. That's a total of four hours down, so it cost them £10,000 in lost revenue. Yet they paid you £135 for the three hours you were on site to fix it. Seems like they got a bargain." Frank raised an eyebrow.

"I hadn't thought about it like that, but I see what you mean. The reality was though, it only cost me my time."

"It cost you much more than just your time, Simon," Frank said with a serious expression fixed across his face. "The five hours you were dealing with this client earned you £135, less the cost of fuel for the hour's journey each way. Firstly, you didn't earn £45 per hour; you actually earned £27 per hour on that job because you weren't paid when you were traveling. Secondly, for that £27 per hour you were unable to generate more business that could have earned you £45. So, each hour you were tied up was costing you rather than benefiting you. Each hour was making it harder to achieve financial security."

Simon was stunned. He could see the logic of Frank's argument. He had simply never looked at his problem in this way before.

"What's more," Frank added. "The amount you did charge the client was only a fraction of what you could have charged them."

"But I can't base my hourly rate on my clients' revenue figures," Simon said defensively. "I can't ask them financial details about their businesses."

"I agree. I'm not suggesting you need to do that."

"Then how can I decide what hourly rate to charge different businesses?"

DESIGNING A NEW MODEL

"You need to think about this is a much better way and design a new model; one that gives you what you really want from your business. Do you remember what that is?"

"Of course! I want financial security," Simon sighed. "Which model will do that for me?"

"Before we decide the model itself, we need to work out what financial security means for you. Do you remember when we first met in the pub and I described financial security as having enough breathing space?

"Our first task, then, is to work out what financial breathing space means for you, personally. How much do you need each month so that all your bills are covered? Not only just covered, but comfortably enough so you can enjoy the pleasures you want. Not a luxurious lifestyle, but one where you can breathe comfortably and where there's no financial pressure anymore. How much would that represent per month?"

Simon thought about what this would look like, but it wasn't difficult to arrive at his figure. In truth, he felt slightly embarrassed at the number and told Frank: "If I'm honest, just £4,000 a month would remove all the pressure."

"Great," said Frank, who didn't seem surprised. "Write that number down in your notebook. That £4,000 is your target number for each month. I want you to become slightly obsessed with this number. Not obsessed, but slightly obsessed, because this will now be the basis for all your business decisions."

"It seems like a long way off right now to be honest," Simon said.

"We're about to change that. Now we know that you want to earn £4,000 a month, the aim is to do that consistently and reliably every single month. Sound good?"

"It would be amazing! How can we do that?"

MATHS OF THE MODEL

"Well, now we can look at the model. Instead of charging by the hour, let's look from a completely different perspective. Start from your objective, which we now know is £4,000 per month. Could you find one business, one client, who would pay you £4,000 a month? Do you think you could find such a client?"

"That sounds like looking for a job that would pay me less than I used to be earning."

"You're right, it would be. I'm not proposing this is your solution, because it wouldn't be a secure business to have. The question is exploring something more important: Can you create an offer valuable enough for a client to pay you £4,000 every single month?"

Frank's Tips 7 – Charging your services by the hour (or day) is a "hard work" Model. The value of your work doesn't depend on how much time it takes, but on the benefit the client receives.

Hourly charging feels comfortable, so is often a difficult model to break. It is worth breaking.

"Well I guess it's possible. I suppose I could. But it feels like a stretch."

"I understand. What's useful is that you can see it as a possibility. Let's go further. Instead of one client paying you £4,000 a month, could you create an offer for two clients to pay you £2,000 a month?"

"I guess that would be a bit easier but it still doesn't feel right having all my eggs in one or two baskets. And it still sounds like having a job."

"What we're doing here, Simon, is finding how you could create offers that are valuable enough for clients to pay you regularly, so you can earn your £4,000 every month much more easily than you're able at the moment. I'm not asking how many hours you can sell.

"We could aim to have one client paying £4,000 a month or you could have two clients paying £2,000 a month. Going further, you could create an offer to attract four clients who'd pay you £1,000 a month. At the other end of the spectrum, you could create an offer to target 40 clients paying you £100 a month and you'd consistently achieve your £4,000 target. See what I mean?"

Table 1: the maths of your Model

Price per month	Number clients	Target per month
£4,000	1	£4,000
£2,000	2	£4,000
£1,000	4	£4,000
£500	8	£4,000
£100	40	£4,000

"I do," said Simon. "I'd be earning what I need, but it would be exhausting working with that number of clients every month."

"Exactly!" said Frank. "You need to identify your sweet spot. Work through the scenarios of how many clients paying you how much per month so you achieve your £4,000 target. The right model for you is a sustainable one that gets you £4,000 a month. Regular, consistent and predictable work created by designing an offer so good that it makes sense for clients to retain your services."

"OK, how do I go about working this out?"

"Back to the notebook. Create three columns on your page. The first column is for the number of new clients you're going to add every month. The middle column is the price you're going to charge them every month and the third column is the number of months they're going to stay with you.

"In this model you'll be winning clients on a recurring income basis; a retainer if you like. This gives you certainty. The purpose of this game is not, 'What can I earn?' The purpose of this game is to achieve financial security. Security means certainty."

"I can do that," said Simon. "Thinking about it, I could even bill some clients a few months in advance as a package rather than charging out per call. At least I'd have a better idea of cash and work coming in."

Frank looked at what Simon was writing down on the notebook, "Looking at the columns on your page," he said. "If you had ten companies paying you £400 each month, does that sound achievable to you? This doesn't mean you'd be only repairing their systems equipment. It might mean you need to be installing equipment, providing a 'prevention service' and you might be teaching and training them how to get more productivity from their existing systems and saving them further investment. You could be creating an offer in any number of ways, as long as your clients would be interested and find it valuable. If they're both, they'll pay for it."

"So, what you're saying is, I need to think about what my clients want and use my skills and resources to create packages that they'll buy?"

"Design your model this way, yes."

Simon paused in thought. He saw the logic in Frank's plan but struggled to see what people would pay him £400 a month for. "It's a big step up from £45 an hour," he said.

"Businesses pay £400 a month for all sorts of things," said Frank. "Insurance, heating, different taxes, marketing, rent – the list is endless. You're getting stuck because you're making this about you. You're asking, 'Why would they pay me £400 a month?' It may sound harsh, but the good news is they don't care about you. They only care about themselves and what they need. They won't take up your offer just because they like you, they'll take up your offer because you're offering something they've realised they'll benefit from.

> **Frank's Tips 8** – Your clients don't care about you, they only care about themselves. Design your model to deliver what they want. When you make it all about you it's harder to find clients to take up your offer. When it's all about them the whole game changes.

"As this is new territory for you, it's natural to have some uncertainty. Any resistance you're feeling is being caused by your own beliefs about whether you're 'worth it' and whether your future clients will be able to pay you. This means it's the perfect time to introduce another of the core principles in the Thrive Framework."

BELIEFS

Frank reached for the paper with the four quadrants set out. He highlighted the 'Self' box again.

"In our last meeting I explained how 'Brain' was the first area for attention in this 'Self' quadrant. Now is the time to introduce the second Self principle: Beliefs. Your beliefs are often hidden, yet they influence how you think, and how you make decisions.

Figure 7: Beliefs in Self Quadrant

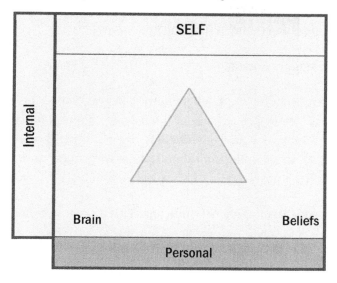

"These are the unconscious programs you're running. They're not always sensible and they're not always true. For example, you may have a belief that £400 per month is unrealistic for your services. This affects your thinking and rules out certain options for your future before you've even tried."

Simon furrowed his brow and Frank could see he needed to explain this to his friend a little deeper.

"Let's assume there are potential clients who could afford to pay. A better question you could ask yourself is: 'What could I offer to make it worth them paying me £400 every month?'

"With your 20 years of experience, I bet you could bring at least £800 of value to their business, don't you think? You could bring them peace of mind, you could add to their financial bottom line and you could bring security to their systems to give them much more confidence and certainty in their operations, right?

"You've already described one company whose system failure had considerable financial impact when it went down. Surely you could offer services worth more than £800 a month?"

"Maybe," Simon conceded.

"I sense you've got a lot of beliefs getting in your way, Simon. Beliefs about work, about pricing, about what your clients think and about what they think of you. Those beliefs are affecting the way you're thinking and, in turn, impacting on the decisions you're making and often not in a good way.

"So right now, it's homework time again. Grab that notebook."

Simon found a blank page. He noticed it was a somewhere approaching the middle of the book by now. His pen hovered over the page.

"I want you to write down this sentence and complete it as many times as you can. "What I believe about _____ is..."

"What's the blank for?"

"Write down that sentence many times and each time with a different word filling the gap. For example, 'What I believe about <u>money</u> is ...'

"You might choose to explore 'pricing', 'customer expectations', or even 'the value of what I do', 'professionalism' or the 'services I offer'. I want you to write down and work out what you believe about each word or phrase you choose. You could even go beyond business and think about what you believe about Susan, your relationship, your strengths, your qualities and even what makes you happy.

"When you get deep into this it can be very revealing. Good or bad, write it down. Become conscious about your beliefs. Then you can see which ones help you and which ones don't. It will help you spot opportunities where you can challenge your own thinking and make better decisions. Oh, and for the bad ones, seek evidence. Chances are, for most beliefs that don't serve you, there is no evidence and the belief is wrong."

"Do you know, Frank, when we first met up again and I thought you could help me with my business, I really didn't expect that we'd be doing so much thinking?" Simon said.

Frank's eyes glinted with enthusiasm. "Thinking is the entire top row in this framework. It's thinking that provides all the answers to all your problems. The thing is Simon that you think you've got a business problem where, in reality, you've got a thinking problem that shows up in your business."

"That sounds quite profound."

"I think you're right," smiled Frank. "I think I'll write that down. Oh, and a bit more homework for you."

Simon looks at him incredulously.

"But you've already started this. I want you to work out your numbers. I want you to decide the number of clients you'd like to add per month. Go further and decide a price you feel is right for an offer you want to create. Remember not to let old thinking get in the way here. I'm looking for you to use the lessons covered today so you come up with new ideas. Your future financial security will be as easy or as tough as the quality of these new ideas."

Frank's Tips 9 – Work out your numbers. It doesn't matter if you don't like numbers, work them out anyway.

"Honestly, Frank, I'm excited but I'm also quite nervous. It sounds like this is a crucial moment for my future and I'm not entirely clear how it will turn out."

"Simon, that is exactly why most people don't think this way and don't change. It seems difficult and the benefit is not immediately obvious. It's much easier to dive in, charge by the hour, try to sell lots of hours and end up in the Busyness Delusion."

"I hate how familiar that sounds!" Simon said. "I'll do the work. Thanks for your help. Shall we meet same time next week?"

"Next Monday it is," said Frank.

Later, as Simon headed back to his kitchen table office, he became lost in thought. He'd always been wrapped up worrying about who would hire him for the next few hours.

But following this conversation with Frank, his thoughts felt much bigger and much more significant for his future.

Frank was right – he did think £400 a month was a lot to ask his clients to pay. After all, he'd been finding it uncomfortable to charge for five hours at £45 even though the client's benefit was much bigger.

He was starting to realise that he did have beliefs he wasn't aware of and he could see how these were affecting his thinking and his confidence.

The week ahead was still "just thinking", but Simon was now enrolled. He could tell the decisions he'd make this week would define his future business.

Quite possibly, it would define the rest of his life.

CHAPTER 4
MIND THE GAP

As the following Monday dawned, Simon was awake before the alarm. This was an unusual experience and not the typical start to his working week.

He was more used to Mondays starting with the frantic screeching of his alarm clock shocking him out of his slumber. Waiting for his pulse to return to its resting rate, his mind would usually race to the ever-increasing list of tasks awaiting his attention. Clients to see, emails to deal with, phone calls to make, money to collect, bills to pay; the list was as relentless as it was necessary. His first challenge normally was to summon enough energy to stick his feet out from under the duvet and eventually get out of bed. Standing upright, he felt he'd already used half the day's supply of willpower. By the time he was dressed and downstairs, he was usually well and truly engrossed in his own mental world of worry and pressure.

But today was different.

After the work he'd done in the last seven days, he was looking forward to sharing his realisations and ideas with Frank. For once, the hands on the clock seemed to moving at a teasing, crawling pace, slowly reaching 9am. This was a very different Monday in Simon's self-employed experience.

He walked briskly to Frank's office, armed with his notebook that, by now, was approaching three-quarters full. He'd never made so many notes in such a short period. He'd realised that he'd never done such deep thinking about his business and his life before. His discoveries were exciting and motivating. He sensed he was building momentum.

As he arrived, Frank was already in reception. From Simon's demeanour it was clear he was keen to get going, so Frank ushered him along the corridor and into his office. They assumed their familiar positions on the sofas.

"Have you worked out your model now?" Frank asked.

"I think I have."

"You think?"

"Well, this is how I see it working: In order to earn £4,000 a month consistently every month, it means I need to have clients who are slightly bigger businesses. It's going to be hard for me to achieve this result working only with one-man bands. I need to be working with businesses with at least 25 staff. For clients of that size I could charge £20 per head per month for IT support and training – around £500 per month in total. For the services I'll be offering, this will still be great value for money for each client. With this pricing, it means I would only need eight clients to achieve my financial security.

"My estimate is that each client would need an average of ten hours of my time in a month. This means I'd be actually delivering my services for only 80 hours a month. There's quite a difference between 80 hours a month and 80 hours a week!"

"That's interesting," Frank said. "The eight clients would give you £4,000 a month, which represents financial security. How long do you think it would take you to win these eight clients?"

"I'd like to gain about three new clients every couple of months," Simon explained. "I think I'd need to approach about 50 businesses to win those three clients. Dealing with that many prospects will take a lot of time and effort, which is why I think it'd take a couple of months to win three."

Table 2: Growth the cumulative way

	Month 1	Month 2	Month 3	Month 4	Month 5	Month 6
Number clients	1.5	3	4.5	6	7.5	9
Monthly price	£500	£500	£500	£500	£500	£500
Monthly Income	£750	£1,500	£2,250	£3,000	£3,750	£4,500

"I like the way you're thinking, Simon. It's clear and it's focused on doing exactly what you need to do to achieve the objective, which is financial security. So, if you do manage to win three of these clients every two months and you need eight in total then you would achieve your financial security number in less than six months. How would that feel?"

"It would be a huge relief," Simon admitted. "It would be amazing. It feels difficult to believe if I'm honest."

"We discussed beliefs last week – you now recognise the impact they have on your future actions," warned Frank.

"You're right. I've become very aware of this. I made notes about it during the week. Look how well used my notebook is already." Simon held it up, and Frank could see how dog-eared the pages looked.

"Simon, this is really great progress. I must congratulate you on everything you've said this morning. It's clear you're starting to see how much easier it can be to reach financial security."

It felt somewhat childish, but Simon beamed with pride.

METHOD

There was more learning ahead though and it was time to get back to the Thrive Framework. Simon had already mentioned a couple of principles Frank hadn't yet covered.

"In the Resources quadrant, I've explained one principle, which is 'Model'," Frank said. "With the progress you've made we can move on to think about the next one, which is 'Method'."

Frank wrote 'Method' on the second point of the triangle.

Figure 8: Method in Resources quadrant

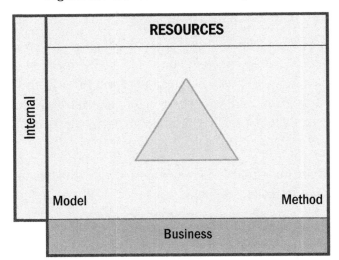

"This 'Method' is your process for consistently delivering the results you promise your clients. How consistent are you with your method for clients in your business as it stands today?"

"I suppose it's fair to say it's ad hoc at the moment," said Simon. "Clients' computers and IT kit break down, they call me and I go out and I fix the problem."

"So, you're reacting to circumstances," Frank replied. "You're not in control of what you are doing or when you do it."

"Well, unless I was in control of when the equipment breaks down, I can't really see how this could change." Simon said.

"Tell me this: Do your clients want their problems fixed?"

"Well of course they do," said Simon, confused at the line of questioning. Frank paused.

"I'd suggest this isn't what they want," he stated.

It left Simon even more puzzled. How could his clients not want to have their problems fixed? But he could see that Frank was ready to explain.

"By the time the problem with their equipment has happened, it's too late," he said. "When they have the problem, sure, they want that problem fixed. And there are many businesses, including yours, who are happy to provide that 'fix' solution. But, when you step back and look at the whole picture, what those businesses really want is for the problems never to happen in the first place, right?"

"Well, I can't argue with that, obviously. But it seems difficult to provide a service to solve a problem that hasn't yet happened," Simon said.

"Last week you told me that one of your clients would lose £2,500 every hour their systems were down."

"Ah, I see where you're coming from now," said Simon. "I can see why avoiding or preventing the problem would be more valuable to the clients. But I'm not sure they'd understand that, though."

"We'll come to how you can get them to understand that in due course, but for now it's worth realising what you just said," said Frank. "You're looking at changing your 'Method' from reactively fixing to proactively preventing problems. How could you do that?"

Simon thought for a while before replying. "I could audit their systems in the first instance, I suppose. As I take them on as a new client, I could check their IT is in good shape. It would be obvious to me when something is likely to cause a problem in the near future. Come to think of it, I've got a checklist I could use for the audit. I can see how I could schedule those audits to suit my time availability rather than everything being an emergency and needing me to drop everything. An audit is never going to be an emergency."

"Yet again, Simon, this is great thinking. And how would this approach affect your work?"

"I can see that I'd have the space, I'd have the time and I'd have the certainty of what I'm doing and when. I wouldn't be running around like a headless chicken."

Frank sat back thoughtfully. Simon looked at him, waiting for the next question.

"If you ran your business like that, how would Susan feel?"

Simon took a deep breath and realised the significance. "It would change everything," he acknowledged.

"Right," said Frank. "So, let's recognise what you're saying. By working in this way, by setting up systems and an offer that creates space for you so that your work could be consistent, it'll give you time for your relationship. It will also give you time to look for more clients and more business, and not to be burnt out at the end of the day and utterly exhausted at the end of the week, relying on the takeaway banquet. And importantly, according to this schedule and plan you'd have financial security within six months and you'd have no more feast and famine."

"You just asked me how Susan would feel and she'd feel relieved, but me – I'd feel ecstatic!"

"Fantastic," said Frank. "Can you go ahead and implement this plan right now?"

"Well, as I said earlier, I only work with really small businesses right now, not these bigger ones with 25-plus staff. So, this is something quite different and I need to work out how to get those clients.

"I guess I need to work out who to approach, what to say to them and what my offer looks like. It's a good job I can use Google properly to at least partly help me out."

"Great. But just before you start googling, this is a chance to fill in some more of the Thrive Framework."

Frank pulled out the by now familiar four boxes and in the 'Self' box he completed the final point of the triangle with the words 'Skills and knowledge'.

Figure 9: Skills and Knowledge in Self quadrant

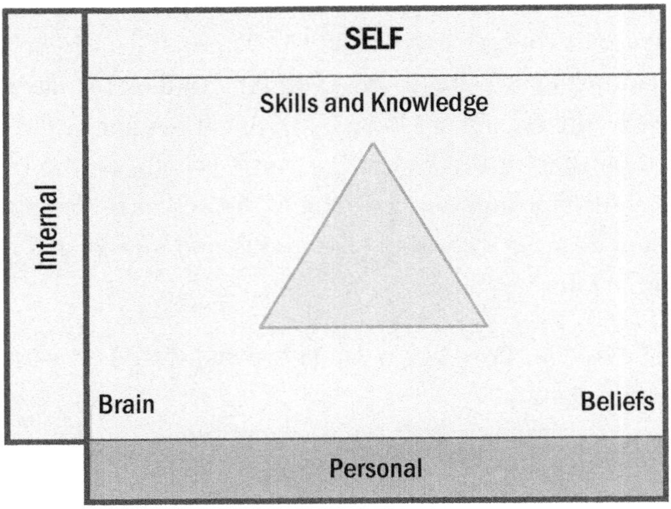

SKILLS AND KNOWLEDGE

"You'll remember, Simon, that this quadrant represents the 'you, personally', as opposed to the 'you, business'. These are the areas to focus on inside your head. We've covered 'Brain' and 'Beliefs'. Now we complete the triangle with 'Skills and Knowledge'. This is because you now need to spend your time working out what you need to know and what you need to be able to do so that when you dive in, your business is going to work.

"Most self-employed people dive straight in and get busy. You now know this is the Busyness Delusion. They don't achieve their aims because they haven't realised their knowledge gaps or skill gaps. And that's because they have no idea of their Reason beyond earning money. With no clear Reason they have no clarity on the Model to get them there – because there isn't a 'there' in the first place.

"Also, they don't consider the Model either. Because 'earning money' is so vague that any model can work. However, any model is unlikely to help them achieve financial security. And because they're not developing a consistent Method, they don't recognise their skills and knowledge gaps. The result is they fall into the Busyness Delusion. You now have the insight that's currently eluding them.

"Your own Skills and Knowledge gaps are likely to include the knowledge of how to get those potential clients to listen to you. How best to approach these prospects? Let's identify what you need to know. What do you need to be able to do?"

Simon thought for a moment. "The first thing is to know how to find those businesses because they're all new to me right now. So, I guess I've got to research where they are. I've got to find out about their current IT systems set-up to help me understand what their real problems are. Google can help me find them. I'm not sure how to do the rest yet."

"OK," said Frank. "You already have questions you're starting to raise. What other questions would you need to answer?"

Simon paused again. "I need to know the best person in the prospect company to speak to. But if I identify them, I'm not sure what to say to them, how to approach them or even how to get them interested in IT support services without being given the cold shoulder."

Frank encouraged him to go on. "Assuming you work that out and you've managed to get into conversation with them, what else do you need to know?"

"I'd need to know how to make a good pitch." As soon as he mentioned the idea of pitching, Simon shuddered. "Frankly, the idea of pitching terrifies me. I hate selling."

"Ah, you're not alone in that," said Frank. "But again, we can come to that in good time."

Simon went on: "I guess there's a whole load of more questions that I need to think about – a load of more knowledge gaps."

"I think you're probably right," said Frank. "Time to make more notes again. What I'd like you to do for your homework this week is to make a note of everything you think you need to know so that you can successfully approach, convince, sell and win the kind of new clients you want to be working with.

"Remember, this future business of yours is going to be one that gives you financial security way more easily that your current business possibly can. You're going to overcome your own Busyness Delusion."

Frank's Tips 10 – Whatever you're trying to achieve with your business, you will have skills and knowledge gaps. Rather than diving in, identify your gaps and decide how to bridge them.

Your progress will be smoother because you'll spend less time doing the wrong things.

"Trust me Frank, I'm no longer under any delusion. You've really made me think," Simon said. "I need to be crystal clear that my 'Method' is feasible and will deliver consistent and reliable client results. Then I can be confident that the service I sell will deliver the goods."

"Brilliantly summarised," said Frank. "That's a great point and one more for your notebook."

"Yet again, I think my head is full for now," laughed Simon. "Let's schedule our next meeting."

"Monday again?" suggested Frank. "I'm really enjoying seeing how you're developing. The work you're doing at this stage is going to make the world of difference to you achieving your financial security. I think you'll be surprised how quickly you'll get there. And it'll be so much simpler than all the efforts you've made in your business so far."

"I'm looking forward to it," Simon said. "In the meantime, I'll get on with this next homework, and I'll see you next Monday."

As Simon strolled home he realised two things.

The first was how differently he felt. Almost all self-employed Monday mornings were the source of angst and worry. These recent Mondays with Frank were changing his experience and his expectations. He sensed he was walking taller. He had more optimism and much more clarity about his future than he'd ever had since starting this venture. As the sun shone down on his back, he felt more in control.

It was true that there were no external results from all the work he'd done with Frank yet. So far, everything was in his head. But this was exactly in line with Frank's Thrive Framework.

However, what had been going on in his head was going to pave the way to a much more secure, calmer and better future. This was a future that Susan was going to love.

The second thing Simon realised was he was going to need another notebook.

Figure 10: Reason, Self and Resources quadrants

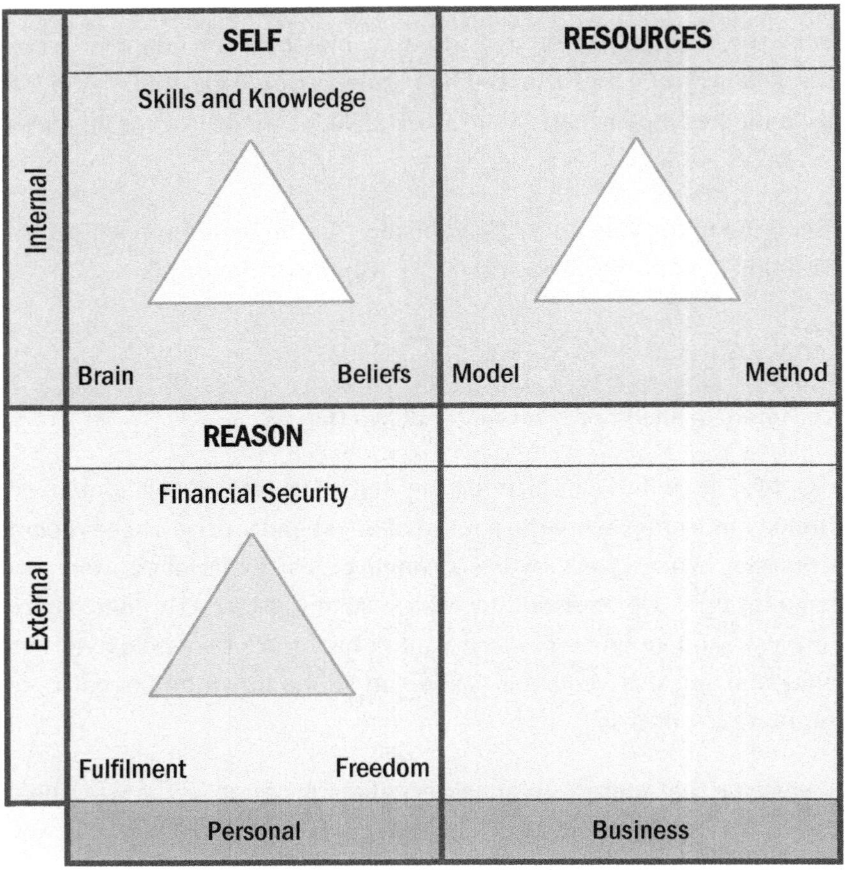

	SELF	RESOURCES
Internal	Skills and Knowledge Brain Beliefs	Model Method
	REASON	
External	Financial Security Fulfilment Freedom	
	Personal	Business

CHAPTER 5
BECOMING ATTRACTIVE

Simon hurried to Frank's office in a buoyant mood the following Monday, as was now becoming a habit.

He'd had an encouraging week. He'd won a satisfying and reassuring amount of work. He certainly felt more confident about how things would pan out – maybe his potential clients could detect that confidence and were therefore more willing to agree to agree to his proposals. Whatever the reason, Simon sensed that something was shifting and his business was starting to take a turn for the better.

Despite the new work and being busy, he had still managed to make time for the planning Frank had asked. He was increasingly excited about the possibility of creating a business that would give him predictable financial security. He did wonder how it would work out in practice rather than just on paper, but he believed he had grounds to be hopeful. He was confident Frank would direct him in the right direction.

As ever, Frank greeted Simon and offered him a coffee before they moved down to his office. He asked Simon how he'd got on with his homework.

"First things first," he said. "I may be as surprised as you are, but I've started my second notebook. I can't believe how many thoughts I've had over the last few weeks and how important this feels."

"What have you realised so far?"

"My task over the last week was to identify where I lack the knowledge in order to put all these plans into practice. So, I've noted where I think I'm OK and then I've noted where I believe I have gaps. The first is how to find these bigger potential clients. I think I am OK with that one. I can use Google and other sources to locate names and places for these types of businesses in my area. I'll be able to find and identify them.

"Next is how to identify their real problems. When I first thought about it I was confident I knew their problems, but now I've thought deeper I'm not sure that's the case. I'm not sure I understand their real problems. Of course I understand the technology issues that they may have, but I have a sense that just solving the tech problems is not really solving their bigger problems and those are the ones that are worth the price I need to charge. So, I'm not sure how to go about researching what their real problems are."

"I'm really impressed with that level of thinking," Frank said. "It would be very easy to assume that you know their problems, even though you haven't spoken with them. You'll be glad to hear the answer of how to research their problems is, of course, is simpler than you think. You need to speak with them. We can talk about how to do that later."

"OK," said Simon. "The next question is how to identify who can make the decision to hire me. I think I know how to go about that, at least as a first attempt, which is searching the companies on LinkedIn and identifying the job titles. I'd also check their website."

"You could even phone and ask," Frank interrupted with a smile, yet making a serious point. Simon held up his hand, acknowledging the simple solution.

"Then I come to the question of how to approach them and not get fobbed off," Simon continued. "The idea of approaching them cold is, frankly, really uncomfortable for me."

Frank stayed quiet. He continued looking calmly at Simon, inviting him to continue.

"OK, the next issue I have is how to make a pitch. It fills me with dread. I hate the idea of selling. I hate people who sell. It has such a bad reputation and I don't want to be tarred with the same brush."

Frank smiled. "You're not the first to have that opinion, Simon, and you won't be the last. And I have a feeling we'll be changing that perspective in today's conversation."

"Sounds promising," said Simon. "My final concern is how to close the sale. I will be offering two services and asking for a price much higher than anything I've tried up to this point. I'm feeling uncomfortable not knowing how to close the sale."

Figure 11: filling in the knowledge gaps

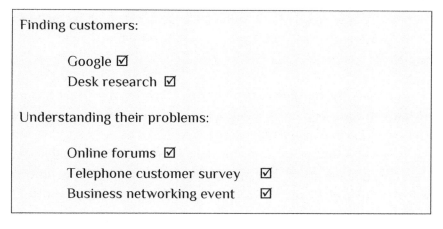

"Simon, I think you've done an excellent job in identifying some of your knowledge gaps," said Frank. "Do you recognise that some of those issues that you've raised are not just knowledge gaps? They're being influenced by one of the other principles we've talked about in the 'Self' quadrant – your Beliefs.

"You have a set of beliefs around how the future client is going to react to your pricing. That belief is influencing how you feel and how you're approaching this piece of work. You have a belief about what selling means and that belief is influencing how you're approaching the sales task. We'll cover all of these, but what strikes me is how you feel comfortable in certain areas and uncomfortable in others. The area of greatest uncertainty is to do with sales and marketing."

"Oh, you're absolutely right," said Simon. "Sales and marketing, I absolutely dread that. I'm a geek because I'm meant to be a geek and geeks don't do selling."

They both laughed at Simon's revelation.

"I suspect there's an element of truth in that for you," Frank replied. "However, it's worth acknowledging that even though you're not earning enough right now, you are bringing in some level of income. The fact is you already have some success in sales. All we need to do is point your focus in a more fruitful direction to get better results."

"I appreciate the confidence you seem to have in me," said Simon. "What you've helped me think about in the last few weeks is, almost literally, mind expanding. It's made me realise that my struggles and average financial results so far are not a reflection on me, but just the consequence of my way of thinking. I've never been taught this way of thinking before, but I can see how useful and important it is."

"Of course I have confidence in you," Frank told him. "In just a few hours together in these last few weeks you've shown how quickly you've picked up the importance of thinking and decision making. The level of thinking you have applied up to this point gives me every indication that you can take the ideas I'm going to share with you today and run with them and be very successful. You're developing insights that will transform your business, your performance and your financial results. You've given me every reason to have confidence in you.

"It's all grounded in the magic of these principles. I've shared these ideas with many people before you. Every single person who's adopted these ideas and applied the lessons has created the life they designed. This happens because these principles work. They are the ingredients I used in building my own businesses and creating a life that inspires me.

"Let's carry on, because there's more for you to learn. Tell me, what specifically are you worried about or uncertain about in relation to sales and marketing?"

Simon thought for a moment. He was basking in Frank's encouragement and the question caught him by surprise.

"I recognise how important sales and marketing are, of course, and I want to get much better and more confident in that part of my business," Simon replied. "I suppose I'm afraid of trying something and it not working. I'm afraid of failing. I'm afraid what people's reaction will be. I'm also wondering how I can afford the time to get better at it given I'm still firefighting and still living hand-to-mouth at the moment.

"From what you taught me in our first meeting, I recognise that that's an emotional reaction. But it genuinely feels like I haven't got much time to get this right."

Frank nodded and encouraged him to continue.

"I'm not stupid. I can see myself in the mirror. I can see that I'm looking haggard and frazzled. I really enjoy coming to these meetings because I find them uplifting and inspiring and they give me hope, but every other day of the week it's really hard graft and I want some shortcuts to get this going."

Frank sat back. "Thanks for your honesty, Simon. You really seem to be aware of your own situation right now. As you've learned, being aware allows you to think more calmly, rationally and clearly, and that is going to enable you to make the decisions you need to make.

"To answer your concern directly we need to look at the resources you have and how we can best use them so you can start to take action. Does that sound good?"

"Absolutely. I need to take action," said Simon.

TME

"Let's go back to the Thrive Framework and fill in some more of the puzzle for you." Frank picked up his pen and added a final label to one of the triangle points in the 'Resources' box. Simon could see he'd written 'TME'. He was none the wiser and wondered what this stood for.

Figure 12: TME in Resources quadrant

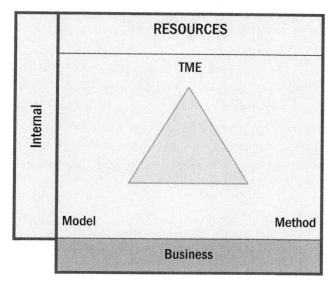

"TME are your available resources," Frank explained. "We all have them – time, money and energy. Yet we use these common resources in very many different ways.

MONEY

"To make sense of this, let's start with the 'M' – money. Tell me, how abundant or how scarce do you think money is?"

"Well that's easy," said Simon. "Money is scarce. It's really difficult to get a hold of. There's never enough to go around."

Frank smiled. "I have yet to find someone who – at this stage – has a different view from you. Everyone thinks money is scarce. There's some good news though. Your answer is wrong."

Simon was puzzled. "What do you mean, wrong? Of course money's scarce!"

"Actually it's not, and I'll explain why. It's difficult to accept at first, because it's so common to believe in its scarcity. That's the trouble with beliefs; they can be very persuasive even when they're not true.

"Here's why I say money is abundant: Look out of this window and see all the buildings. They are all businesses. There's money tied up and flowing in every single one of those businesses. Picture all the houses in the area where you live. There's money flowing around in all of those households. Expand that picture to a wider area, a county or a national scale. There's money flowing around everywhere. Money, itself, is everywhere.

"All you need to do is access it somehow. Of course, I realise that you don't yet recognise money is abundant and everywhere. You look into your bank account and it tells you a different story. But when I talk about money I'm not referring to your personal bank account. I'm pointing out that money is flowing everywhere and it's a resource you can access. It is limitless. It has no end. It is truly abundant."

Simon liked the idea in theory, but couldn't see how he could access other people's money in reality.

"Again," Frank continued. "That's a belief I'd like to smash for you, because actually you can access money from all sorts of places. For example, given that you are the geek that you profess, I imagine you have many gadgets at home, some of which have been collecting dust for some time now."

Simon looked slightly sheepish and thought that Susan would agree with Frank.

"If you sold some of those gadgets, what would you have?"

"Fewer gadgets," joked Simon. "But yes, I'd have more money. I'd rather not sell them, though."

"Naturally, you'd rather not sell them. I'm not surprised, but that's not the point. The point is you can turn those gadgets into money. This is the principle. I only use those gadgets as an example. There are all sorts of assets which you could sell or even lease that would increase your access to money. Then money becomes a resource. Selling assets is only one way to get access to the money. Other examples include borrowing it or to getting people to invest in your ideas.

> **Frank's Tips 11** – Money is neither scarce nor limited. Your access to money is only constrained by the limit of your thinking.

"Access to money is only constrained by the limit of your thinking. This is why I say money is a limitless resource. But because you think money is scarce, you hold onto it. And instead, you throw other resources at your problem. Those other resources are the T and the E.

TIME

"The first of those is T – time. Would you say you've been throwing time at your problems?"

"I guess you could say that," Simon answered. "It's just me trying to solve everything and do everything myself."

"Exactly," Frank looked pleased with Simon's answer. "How much time do you have?"

"Not enough!" he exclaimed.

"Isn't that quite a statement?" Frank asked. "You already don't have enough hours to do everything you believe you should be doing. And specifically, how much time do you have?"

"The same as everyone else, I suppose," admitted Simon.

"Right. How much?"

"24 hours every day," Simon replied.

"Some of which you need for working. Some of which you'll need for admin to keep on top of the business. Some of which you need to have a great relationship with Susan and the kids. And some of which you need to just to get some sleep, right?"

"Sure. It doesn't seem like I have enough time in a day even for just business."

"I'm not surprised. The point is that time is a scarce resource. We all have the same amount and it's finite. This is very different from money. As I've already explained, money is not finite. Time, on the other hand, is most definitely finite.

"So yes, time is a scarce resource. To some extent you can expand the amount of time as a resource by getting other people to help you. This is known as using other people's time. Then you have more people working in your business and helping to solve your problems. But recognise the resources in that situation. You're using your money resource to buy their time resource. Hence, you can use money to increase time resource available."

Simon thought for a while. "Again, I can see what you're saying, Frank, and it does make sense. But I just don't have the available money right now. If I did, I wouldn't want to spend it on other people's time. I'd rather do things myself."

"And that, Simon, is exactly why you're struggling so much. You're trying to do everything yourself. You're relying on a resource that is finite in its capacity."

> **Frank's Tips 12** – Business becomes a struggle when you rely on resources with finite capacity. There is no law that requires it to be a struggle.

Frank continued: "It's fair to say this is a rational decision. I'm not saying it's a stupid thing to do – it's a very common thing to do – but there are consequences. When you understand the trade-offs you're making between time and money, you can become more skilful at making better decisions for your situation. At the moment you're prioritising the use of your time resource over the use of your money resource and for understandable reasons.

"To make your time resource valuable you need to be productive and useful, so you use it well. Does that make sense?"

Simon was quiet; listening. He could see this was another way of seeing the world and one with very significant implications. Somehow, Frank had a way of thinking that had eluded Simon so far. "Sure, of course it makes sense."

"Those are the hidden realities behind money and time. Now let's look at the third resource, which is the E – energy.

ENERGY

"Energy is the most fragile of the three resources available to us all. For example, how does your mood affect your energy?"

"Oh, well that's easy to answer. When I'm in either a bad mood or stressed, I know that I feel run down."

> **Frank's Tips 13** – When your business depends on your energy to drive forward, it is set up in the most fragile way possible. Remember, you have unlimited access to infinite resources. You don't have to rely on your own energy.

"Precisely. Yet to make your business successful you've admitted to wanting to do everything yourself. In other words, you're relying on your energy resource. You're designing your business to be dependent on the most fragile of resources that you have. You depend on having enough energy to keep things going and keep it working well. If you're going to continue this way, it's important that you're resilient. How can you make yourself resilient?"

"Well, maybe if I drink more coffee? Will that help?"

"Nice try," Frank laughed. "You can make yourself more resilient by having more control over how you think and how you respond. We've already talked about this – it's everything in the 'Self' quadrant in the Thrive Framework. All the answers you need, for your life and for your business, lay in the responses to your thinking around that top row.

"I asked you to design a 'Model' and a 'Method' and to look at the 'Skills and Knowledge' you need. I tackled and challenged you on your 'Beliefs' and you're already demonstrating that you can have much better control over your 'Brain' and how you think. And now you need to recognise you are making decisions about the three 'TME' resources. You need to find your best allocation of those resources. As with everything we've covered so far, this is directly linked to your skill in making decisions. You need to make decisions wisely."

"OK," said Simon. "So I'm confident in the Model that I'm designing and I know the Method works because I used to do this work. I had checklists and everything else that I've designed in my last job. I suppose I can get a few books and ask around for the other knowledge gaps to do with that."

He paused, furrowing his brow. "But I'm still worried about getting those eight clients even with all that extra knowledge and understanding. I still have to step outside my comfort zone into what seems like a very hostile place for me."

"Let's look at your options," Frank replied. "You can try to learn about sales and marketing from books and other resources, relying only on yourself. That's using your time and energy. Another option is to get someone to do the sales and marketing for you, which is using the money resource.

"Alternatively, you can get someone else who knows how to do this to teach you and speed up your learning. If only you knew someone who knew a thing or two about this subject!" Frank winked.

"As if it were planned," he continued. "This brings us to the final quadrant in the Thrive Framework. The one that's still empty. Shall we have a look at what that contains?"

"Well, I'm assuming this final quadrant covers sales and marketing then?" said Simon.

MOMENTUM

Frank reached for the piece of paper and drew a triangle in the final quadrant, matching the other three. He labelled the quadrant 'Momentum'.

'Momentum,' Simon thought. 'It's not sales and marketing, but it sounds encouraging.'

LSD

Having written the word, Frank explained to his friend what it meant: "I refer to the three principles in this quadrant as LSD. Not the LSD the Beatles used to sing about, though. Instead it's 'Leads', 'Sales' and 'Delivery'.

Figure 13: Momentum quadrant

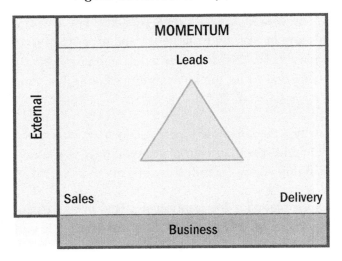

"I'm aware you're uncomfortable with these topics, but once we get through what I'm going to show you now, you'll realise that winning eight clients is a whole lot easier than you feared. The reason people find sales and marketing so difficult is because they start with the wrong focus. They start by looking for people who are ready to buy."

"That sounds like a very sensible approach," Simon suggested.

"Yes, it does seem sensible. However, there's a problem with this focus – no one knows who those 'ready buyers' are and it's very competitive looking for them. Let me explain.

"I'd like to picture your entire potential market inside another triangle. The area inside that triangle represents 100 per cent of all the people and businesses you could possibly work with."

Figure 14: 100% of potential market

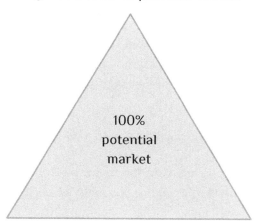

"Whether they know me or not?" asked Simon.

"That's right," confirmed Frank. "Not just the potential clients you may already know, but any potential client. In other words, our initial sales and marketing plans are not restricted. At this early stage we remain open to all potential clients, whether we know them or not and whether they know of us or not."

"In that case, that's a very big market," Simon said.

"And isn't that a great place to start from?" smiled Frank.

"Well, yes, but there are too many potential clients to target. Surely I should narrow down and focus on the few I believe already need me?"

"By definition, they all would benefit from working with you," Frank said. "This 100 per cent is the market that has the problem your Method solves. All being well, there are too many businesses in your market. As a consequence, the natural approach would be to try to find the 'ready buyers'. This is what most early-stage businesses do. But when they try, they immediately come up against the next marketing challenge of who to contact and what to say."

"Sounds horribly familiar," Simon agreed.

"It's worse than you think,' warned Frank. "Typically, these marketing messages sound like this: *'Is this you? We do this! Want to hire us?'* When you put this kind of message out into your market, it's too early."

"What do you mean, 'too early'?" Simon asked.

"It means the person receiving the message isn't ready to respond right then. They need much more warming up beforehand."

"In which case, why do people try this approach so often?" Simon was perplexed.

"Because they're focusing on themselves rather than on their potential client and because they're afraid of their competitors," Frank told him. "They're all hunting for the same prospects, so competition is hectic and the pressure's high."

"That's just inevitable though, isn't it?" Simon asked. "There's always going to be competition, right?"

THE FIRST 3%

"Unless we take a different approach, yes. In this triangle of 100 per cent of your potential market, we first consider the top three per cent. As a general rule, in any market there are around three per cent of prospects who are thinking, 'I know what my problem is, I know the solution and I'm just trying to decide who I should buy it from.'

Figure 15: 3%, 7%, 90% view of potential market

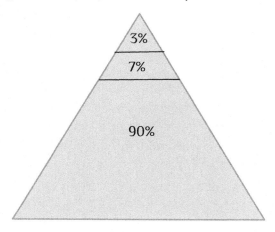

"Now, Simon, would you like to speak with those people?"

"Of course I would. They are ready to buy."

"Precisely. They're ready to buy, so you want to find them. The trouble is that everyone else also wants to speak to those people because they're ready to buy. But there are two practical challenges. The first is that these prospects are not walking around with a flag over their head saying, 'I'm ready to buy', which makes it very difficult to know who those three per cent are. How do we identify them?

> **Frank's Tips 14** – As a general rule, in market at any time there are around three per cent of prospects thinking, 'I know my problem, I know the solution and I just need to decide who to buy it from.'

"The second challenge is the high level of competition. Everyone's after them because they're ready to buy. And high competition usually creates a downward pressure on prices. Unless you're careful, winning this kind of competitive business becomes less profitable, which then makes it harder to achieve financial security."

"A double-whammy of bad news." Simon's wry tone revealed his nervousness. "I must admit, I'm now unsure what to do, because these are the people who are going to buy quickest and now you're saying by focusing on them that it's going be harder to get financial security."

"That's not quite what I'm saying," corrected Frank. "What I'm saying is it's natural for everyone to chase these ready-to-buy prospects, but they only account for three per cent of the whole possible market. There are more.

THE NEXT 7%

"Let's look at the next slice. In most markets, at any point in time the next section of around seven per cent of prospects is saying: 'I know my problem, but I don't yet know what the solution is.' Now, would you like to speak to these people?"

"Well of course I would, as they already know that they've got some kind of need that I can solve."

> **Frank's Tips 15** – As a general rule, in any market at any time, there are around seven per cent of prospects thinking, 'I know my problem and I'd like to find the solution.'

"Absolutely. This makes sense doesn't it?" said Frank. "They're looking for an answer and you want to be the one solving their problem. But just as with the top three per cent, these prospects are not walking around with a flag over their head. Who exactly are they? How do we identify them? Again, everyone else is hunting for them too, which again creates a very competitive environment.

"That combined ten per cent at the top of your potential market is being saturated with competing sales and marketing activities. They're bombarded with messages such as, 'Is this you? Then call me'. Tell me, Simon, when you see adverts or receive messages saying, 'If you've got this problem, we should speak' do you pick up the phone and welcome them in?"

"No, I never would to be honest," Simon admitted.

"Of course you wouldn't. And yet the competition spends their time, money and energy chasing that ten per cent.

THE MAJORITY 90%

"But what about the rest of the triangle? This is 90 per cent of your potential market and there's little competition there."

Simon sat up in his chair. He sensed he was about to find out something vital to his future success. But he needed to check something: "You're saying there's little competition for 90 per cent of my potential market?"

"Be mindful to keep your beliefs in check," Frank reminded him. Simon was starting to see how these principles were core to Frank's approach. He also recognised the level of success they'd brought him both in business and in life.

Frank continued: "Those 90 per cent are thinking, 'What problem?' In other words, they're not yet aware they have the problem that you can solve."

> **Frank's Tips 16** – As a general rule, in any market at any time, around 90 per cent of prospects don't yet realise they have the problem you solve. This is where your gold is.

Simon was stumped. "What use are those people to me if they don't know they've got the problem? They don't think they need me."

"That's not what I said," Frank retorted. "I said those 90 per cent don't yet know they have the problem you solve. And getting them to be aware of the problem is where the gold lies.

"Those 90 per cent are not looking. Those 90 per cent are not responding to an advert that says, 'Hey, have you got this problem, let's speak'. Nobody else is competing for their attention because they can't get it.

"However, those 90 per cent are still at risk of having the problem but they just don't know it. What if a company didn't know their virus protection was inadequate? What if an organisation didn't know their entire operation was at risk because of the nature of the IT equipment they're currently using? Do you think if they became aware then they'd start listening to what you had to say?"

Simon paused. He knew what Frank was saying, but his own experience was different. "I've found people aren't chomping at the bit to get into conversations about anti-virus protection and IT infrastructure, especially at parties," he replied, only half-joking. "It's not easy to get people interested in this subject."

"I can imagine you're right. It's not the most obvious ice-breaker. But what if there was a way of attracting the attention of that 90 per cent? What if there was a way to raise their awareness of their problem? In that situation you'd have very little competition, because everyone else is fighting over the ten per cent. If you're the one who has the attention of someone in the 90 per cent, you become the only provider of the solution they need."

Simon was lost in thought. He knew Frank was right. He recognised all the symptoms. He'd been guilty of sending out adverts imploring people to 'Call me!'. He kicked himself for being so naïve.

Then he imagined being the single trusted advisor to a client with a big budget. With trust, he'd lock out any competitors. He'd be preventing problems arising so the client continued to operate smoothly. He wouldn't be stressed, he'd be in control. He'd be charging a regular monthly fee, which would be good value to the client and would create financial security for Simon, Susan and their kids. With everything working so smoothly he'd be able to treat the family to a helicopter ride they'd never experienced before. He'd be financially secure and fulfilled. This would feel incredible. He desperately wanted this feeling.

He snapped out of his reverie, realising he didn't know the first step. "So how do I open the door to those 90 per cent when they don't know that they need me?"

ATTRACTING THE 90%

"I'm going to go back and explain how you will be able to attract the 90 per cent of the market who don't yet know that they have a problem and then you'll see how leads and sales work in this 'Momentum' quadrant. First I'd like to help you understand what's called the customer journey or the buyer journey."

Frank reached for a new sheet of paper and he wrote across it three letters in three columns – A, I and C.

AWARENESS, INFORMATION, CONVERSION

"Remember these letters, because they'll change your marketing for ever," Frank promised. "They stand for 'Awareness', 'Information' and 'Conversion'.

"Imagine a spectrum from left to right. At the left-hand end, you have a stranger. They don't know you and you don't know them. Then at the right-hand end is a paying client.

"To take them on their journey from the left to the right, from stranger to client, they need to go through Awareness, Information and Conversion. This is an approach that has worked for decades. And nowadays, with so many people distracted by internet tactics, this approach is working better than ever. Internet tools and technology can magnify reach, but without understanding the principles people end up floundering and trapped in the Busyness Delusion. Those of us who use the fundamentals have a heavy competitive advantage.

"This approach will help you to attract the people you want to attract. And keep in mind you only need eight clients to give you your financial security."

Simon had learned to trust Frank. The idea of having a competitive advantage and marketing being easy increased his confidence. He waited for the details Frank was about to share.

AWARENESS

"Stage one, then, is Awareness. This is where the stranger – the 90 per cent in this case – become aware. Importantly, I'm not talking about awareness of you; rather they become aware of their problem. More significantly, they become aware of the consequences of that problem.

"When you start looking at how to raise their awareness, it's normal to think the answer is in the medium. It isn't. You can use any and every medium you can think of. If you're online, you could write blog articles or create videos to post on social media. Offline, you could hold seminars, give talks or be a guest speaker. You could post in newsletters or magazines. You could send direct mail. You can even open conversations with individuals at events, on a plane or in a supermarket. I've had surprisingly fruitful conversations just from bumping into someone while out walking the dog.

"All of these mediums and platforms can work, but they don't determine your success. Don't become fixated on finding the ideal medium. When you tune in, you'll realise that clients are everywhere. The key is to have a clear message that helps them understand what their problem is.

"One of the most effective ways to do this is to tell stories. Tell stories about companies who've experienced the same kind of problem as your target market. Explain the consequences of the problem and the impact of solving it. Talk about people like them. You want to provoke the reaction, 'This sounds just like me!'

"Don't talk about you. They don't care about you. They only care about themselves. It's not personal; it's how we all work. When you describe someone else's situation that is just like their own, the message slips through their own filters.

"In the Awareness phase, the aim is to create an emotional response. Whatever their role and situation, they're still human beings and human beings are emotional creatures. We're all impacted from our mammalian brains.

Frank's Tips 17 – A clear message (rather than the medium) is the key to successful marketing. Use stories to demonstrate the prospect's problem and its consequences.

"Every buying decision is, at its root, an emotional decision. It doesn't matter whether you're buying a bottle of water or your next house; your emotions are the dominant influence.

"Naturally, emotions aren't the whole story and I'll get to that in a moment. But it's crucial you understand this Awareness phase. Your objective is to create an emotional response. Effectively, you're secretly and simply tapping into the natural way their brain works.

Frank's Tips 18 – The goal of the Awareness phase is to move your prospect to the conclusion, 'That sounds exactly like me! I need to find out more.'

"You've already experienced how this works. When we met in the pub on that Friday evening a few weeks ago, you wanted to find out more. That led into these series of meetings and the progress you're making. So, stage one is the Awareness stage."

"This is fascinating," beamed Simon. "I'd never thought about it like this before, but now you've pointed it out it's obvious. I admit that my marketing has been trying to attract the ten per cent and I had no idea this was happening. It's no wonder I was getting such low interest. The truth is that I was just copying what everyone else was doing."

"And isn't that great?" Frank interrupted.

"What's great?" Simon asked.

"Everyone else is copying everyone else, which means everyone else is getting the same results as everyone else. The competition has no idea what it's doing and you can steal a march by attracting the 90 per cent they're busily ignoring."

Simon sat back, stunned. "You know Frank, I have never felt this much desire to get going. The idea that my competitors are busy doing the wrong things gives me huge hope."

"See what I mean by the Busyness Delusion?" asked Frank.

"It's so clear now!" Simon.

"But before you get too carried away, I've only explained stage one of this part. Stage two is Information.

INFORMATION

"This is where your prospect wants to find out more. A few minutes ago, I explained that people make their buying decision emotionally. However, often those emotions are not enough to feel confident with the decision. Here's why.

"When they make their decision, they play a movie scenario in their brain. The main scene in that movie is, 'Will I regret this decision?'. They're afraid it may be a silly decision. They're worried about looking foolish to someone else – it's pure mammalian brain in action. Therefore, they also need a rational case to convince and reassure them this buying decision isn't silly. This is what stage two, the Information stage, is all about.

"Essentially, you've helped move them from the 90 per cent who are not aware of their problem into the seven per cent where they're now interested to find the solution. The information you share in stage two needs to reassure them that this solution makes sense. You'll now realise that this stage is connecting with the rational part of their brain – the human brain.

"The Awareness phase is talking to the heart, the emotions and the mammalian brain. The Information phase is talking to the rational, logical and creative human brain.

Frank's Tips 19 – Explaining the rational basis to your solution is often necessary, but only after the prospect has made the emotional connection to want to find out more. They don't need to know how it works. Instead, explain why your Method has the structure you've created.

"And this is where your Method comes into play," Frank continued. "When it's so clearly structured it makes the Information phase easy, because your Method will have a natural process. It will be built on the steps that are logically required. Your Method has a rational basis.

"In your Information stage content, you can explain why you have each step in your Method. You don't need to explain the content of each step. That detail doesn't help their buying decision. What they want is reassurance that it's a sensible decision. You do this by helping them to understand why your Method works. When you've done stage two well, they will respond, 'This makes sense, I need to speak to Simon'.

> **Frank's Tips 20** – The goal of the Information phase is to help your prospect reach the rational conclusion, 'This makes sense. I need to speak to this person.'

"And that's your perfect scenario, because it means you're in the third stage – Conversion. This is where you have your sales conversation."

CONVERSION

This was the part Simon hated and he told Frank so.

"You and most other self-employed people," chuckled Frank. "This is because of your beliefs around selling. It's time to look at it in a very different way."

"When you speak, Frank, I end up looking at everything in a different way," said Simon.

"I'll take that as a compliment," smiled Frank. "I've found most self-employed people have sales conversations in a very random and ad hoc fashion. They don't follow a structure. At best, this is inefficient for improving conversion rates. At worst, it leads to failure. Having no structure makes it hard to learn and hard to get better. Their Skills and Knowledge gaps stay wide. However, if you can master the selling approach then your financial security is almost guaranteed.

"After that you can achieve way more than just security, which is why it's vital to have a structure to your sales conversations.

"One secret to making this effective and to actually enjoy these sales conversations is to use the principle that you're diagnosing, not selling. Your potential client has no need to become your client unless they're suffering from the problem you solve.

Frank's Tips 21 – Unless you have a defined structure to your sales conversation, it's practically impossible to learn. Therefore, it's practically impossible to improve reliably. Define your approach and follow it so you can improve it.

"They don't become your client just because they like you. In blunt terms, as I've said before, they don't care about you. They don't even care how awesome you are, yet this is the basis most self-employed people try to promote.

"Your potential client only cares about having their problem solved in a way that makes them feel confident and reassured. So the sales conversation is not about you, it is about them. Their problem and the solution you bring – not you personally."

Simon shook his head. He'd been making the mistake Frank had just explained. "I can see in every sales conversation I've had so far I've been trying to explain and promote myself," he admitted. "I've wanted to show how much skill I have because I've got 20 years' experience under my belt."

"Exactly," said Frank. "This is so common. It's so natural and understandable. You've become an expert in your area and you want to demonstrate to your potential clients the fact that you are an expert. You want to impress them.

"The good news is that selling can be much easier than that. You don't need to impress them. You need to give them the assurance that the solution you provide will solve the problem they're experiencing. It's as simple as that."

"That sounds encouraging, but how do I do that?"

"Here's a structure that's had impressive results. First, you diagnose their problem. Do not sell, merely diagnose. Ask questions to get them to describe their problem. Once they've described what their problem is, you can ask what outcome they want. In other words, what will it look like when the problem is solved? They have now told themselves what the outcome looks like rather than you.

"Then you help them realise that they can't solve it themselves and therefore they need help. Then you can invite them to understand your solution. This is where they learn how you fix what they've told themselves they need fixing. Invite them to ask questions to understand how your method delivers the result they want. The aim is to help them make the best decision for themselves. It's all about them achieving the result they want.

"This is fundamentally different from what people think of as 'selling'. This is not shifting second-hand cars or double glazing. This doesn't feel like selling – it feels like you're genuinely helping, which is exactly what you are doing. You're helping them to make the very best decision for themselves. When they've decided they need their problem solving, you've been of valuable service already. All that's left is to invite them to ask for your support."

Simon thought for a while before responding. "Frank, that sounds great. I can see the difference between promoting myself and instead offering a solution to fix a problem. I can see why it's less pressure and I can even imagine that when they say, 'No, I don't need it' that it's not personal to me because they're really saying they don't need their problem solved. But I still feel anxious about putting out those messages to the 90 per cent and getting the ball rolling."

Frank leaned forward with reassurance. "I can understand why you would feel worried about that. Instinctively, most people's messages are along the lines of, 'Buy from me, I'm awesome', which feels like you're putting yourself out to be judged.

"But when you take the approach of, 'Tell me about your problem, I have a method to solve that problem and would you like to hear about it?' it's easier and much more natural. They're judging the problem and the Method, not judging you.

"Of course, it's quite normal to be uncomfortable with selling. It goes right back to the mammalian brain. You remember the worst thing that can happen to a mammal? Being judged and sent away from the pack? Being disconnected? Your mammalian brain hates the idea of being judged. Your brain's job is to protect you and being judged opens up a sense of threat. When a potential client turns you down, you feel judged. It triggers your emotional reaction. It feels bad.

"On the other hand, the diagnostic approach creates no judgement about you. It's all about them, their problem and your method. Hence, they're not judging you. And, by the way, think about it from their perspective. They may be worried that an expert is coming along and judging them for getting in the mess that they're in in the first place. So this diagnosis method is better for everybody involved in the conversation.

"When you tell stories that describe how other people have the problem you're solving, they already know they're not the only ones to be suffering from it. You're showing how you can help people and diagnose their problems. When you do that, people will want to connect and contact you."

Simon sat back.

"I have to say, Frank, I used to think I understood how business worked and the rules that you had to follow. And here's another conversation with you which makes me question everything I've been doing. I'm frustrated how hard it's been for the last three years. I've been working such long hours and not achieved the results. As you describe these ideas, it seems so obvious where I've been going wrong!"

"It's not your fault, Simon," Frank said. "Almost everyone falls into this trap. We grew up learning by watching others and then copying what they were doing. When people start a business of their own, there's so much to learn. The most obvious solution is to look around at what others are doing and do the same thing. It's only when you question whether everyone else is getting good results do you wake up from the Busyness Delusion. Yet when you do wake up and learn smarter, easier and more natural methods, you find that achieving financial security is much simpler than you feared.

"It all starts with the top row of the Thrive Framework − it starts inside your own head. It starts with better thinking and better decisions."

"I haven't put this into place yet, but already I'm feeling very grateful for these insights, Frank," Simon replied.

"I appreciate the comment but, as you say, you haven't yet put this into action. It's time to do that now."

Simon nodded. "Definitely. I understand how to create Awareness and explain with Information how my Method works. I Believe I can create an effective structure for a sales conversation.

Table 3: Summary of AIC

Awareness (90%)	Information (7%)	Conversion (3%)
Provoke emotional response, "That's me too! I should find out more."	Provoke understanding response, "This makes sense and is plausible. I should speak to them."	Provoke commitment response, "I no longer want this problem and I am ready to invest in fixing it."
Tell stories and give examples highlighting the problem and its consequences. Provide inspiration that a solution exists.	Give an explanation of why the solution is structured this way.	Design a structured approach to the sales conversation.
Single objective: Move ahead in the AIC journey	Single objective: Move ahead in the AIC journey	Single objective: Win new client

"But I'm just wondering, in the Momentum quadrant of the Thrive Framework you've explained Leads and Sales. What about the final area? Delivery?"

DELIVERY

"Let me ask you a question about this," Frank continued. "What is the objective of what you deliver in your business?"

"Ah, well, that's easy. It's to solve the client's problems."

"Close, Simon, but that's not quite the purpose of the delivery."

"How could it not be the purpose?" asked Simon.

"The objective of the work you do is, of course, to solve the client's problems but the purpose of delivery in this part of the framework is actually to retain your clients."

> **Frank's Tips 22** – The real purpose of delivering your solution to your clients is to retain your clients. Think about it.

Simon thought about this for a minute. "Oh wow. You're completely right, because if I lose customers I'm going to need to find more and more clients to keep filling the coffers to keep my financial security going."

"I've said it before Simon and I'll say it again, you're a fast learner. You join the dots quickly. Of course, if your Method wasn't successful and you didn't solve your clients' problems, then you'd be out of business fairly quickly. So solving the problems is an essential part of the delivery. However, when you think in terms of the Momentum quadrant of the framework, the longer you can retain clients the greater your financial security will be. What's more, you'll find you need fewer clients to sustain that financial security.

"Your method of delivery becomes not only an operational procedure, but also a marketing function. The aim is to retain the clients you're working with."

"I can see this adds a different focus beyond 'doing the work'," said Simon. "I suppose I'd need to follow up with clients to make sure that they're happy with the service."

"Absolutely," confirmed Frank. "Keeping in touch with them not only allows you to make sure they continue to be happy with the service so you retain them longer, it also gives you the opportunity to diagnose new problems they're experiencing and then build that into your existing Method. You're creating more opportunities to sell them more services. Or, more accurately, you're making yourself more valuable to them."

"I love this way of thinking," said Simon.

"Now you have the full picture," said Frank, sitting back and sounding relieved. "This was the final element of the diagram. We've covered everything at least once. There's a huge amount to absorb and you'll need to practise and refresh your thinking as you go, but I can help keep you on track when you need it. But, first things first, you know what happens now?"

"Homework time?" asked Simon.

"Homework time," confirmed Frank. "I want you to go and find the 50 people you said you'll need in order to create your first clients for this new offer. Attract 50 people with your Awareness messages and take them through the AIC phases to convert at least three of them into clients in the next two months. Remember, you said winning three new clients every two months means you'd achieve financial security in less than six months. Now is the time to go out there and put all of this into practice.

"Design your messages, attract your prospects, build their awareness, give them the information and have sales conversations with them. You've got plenty of time, now is the time to go."

As he listened to the homework instructions, Simon detected something in Frank's tone that he couldn't put his finger on. It sounded like Frank was issuing a challenge, perhaps. Maybe he didn't expect Simon to succeed. Maybe, instead, Frank sounded like he'd miss these weekly meetings.

Either way, Simon was fired up and ready to get going. He realised he couldn't hide behind a screen doing endless research anymore. Now was the time to get out into the market. Now was the time to start creating the new kinds of clients that would give him financial security.

In the past, this would have absolutely terrified him. He really did hate the idea of selling. Maybe this helped him feel so comfortable behind a screen or dealing with technology. But today he felt different. It really was remarkable. He was ready to take his business to a different market and move up a level. He was equipped with the ideas and methods to be successful. He could see how he'd made it so hard for so long. It was a small crumb of comfort to recognise how many other self-employed people were going to continue in their own struggle, because they weren't exposed to these ideas and this transformative way of thinking.

Two months.

He had two months to prove that he could put this into practice and report back to Frank. He was determined to make this work.

Now was his time. This was his moment. He was ready.

CHAPTER 6
NOT QUITE ON PLAN

Two months later it was time for Simon and Frank to get together again.

Instead of meeting at Frank's office, they had arranged to be on Simon's home territory. Frank had suggested this venue for two reasons. Firstly, because he wanted to see how things worked in Simon's office and, secondly, because he wanted visible clues as to how Simon was actually performing.

On the drive from his own home, Frank reflected on their conversations over the previous weeks. Simon's proposed new Model along with his improved Method seemed realistic. Simon appeared confident with how to build Momentum and seemed motivated and focused when they left the last conversation.

Frank had seen Simon post a few articles on LinkedIn that did cause him some concerns. The ones about antivirus software were a bit dry. Frank's expectations were for zero or low engagement and he was concerned that Simon was falling into the same busyness trap. However, from what he'd seen online, it was clear that Simon was persevering and hadn't just thrown the towel in.

He was still hopeful, because the principles he had taught Simon had created the 3Fs for many other business owners over the years. It was just a question of whether Simon could apply them successfully himself or whether he needs more intervention.

However, he did have one major concern. Despite Frank's open invitation, Simon had not asked for any help, guidance or input during these last two months. Frank knew from experience that when someone doesn't get in touch and instead tries to work everything out alone that it's a sign they're stuck and probably staying stuck.

He knew that being too proud to ask for help was a serious Achilles heel for a serious business owner. Determined isolation was usually a debilitating burden that too often scuppered enough progress.

Frank had seen too many people refuse to come up for air, usually remaining trapped in their own heads. It was time for him to find out if Simon had indeed stayed stuck.

He pulled into Simon's driveway, stepped down from the raised driver's seat and crunched across the gravel to the front door. He rang the doorbell, stepped back and waited in anticipation of the atmosphere once the door opened.

Susan answered, swinging the door open and warmly welcoming Frank inside. "I'm heading to the shops," she told him. "I thought I'd give you two time and space to go through what's been happening. I know Simon is anxious to get your feedback."

Frank wasn't yet sure what results to expect. Susan called Simon through.

"Frank! It's great to see you again," said Simon, warmly. Frank detected a sense of relief in Simon, but still wasn't sure what his friend had in store. Susan closed the front door behind her and Simon led them both through to his office, which also doubled as the kitchen table.

"Thank you for coming around to see me for a change, Frank," Simon said. "I expect you want to know what's been happening in the last two months."

"Well, I know you were hopeful and positive after our last conversation and I set you that challenge to get your first three clients with your new method and your new offer," Frank replied. "We wanted you to be a third of your way towards your first F – financial security."

"Yes, that was indeed your challenge. And you're right I was hopeful, but I have to admit that I haven't got three clients."

"Oh! OK," said Frank, "Let's see what happened and how I can help you. Tell me more."

STACKING UP THE TOP ROW

Simon shuffled in his seat and began: "As you suggested, the first thing I did was check my model, my method, and my time, money and energy resources, and they all stacked up. I could see how it was going to be possible to create the time and have the structured offer that would work. Combining all these, they would give me the financial security that I wanted.

"I felt it would work but, as I shared with you last time, I wasn't sure how. I didn't have complete certainty, but I knew when I got started things would become clearer. I recognised I just had to overcome my fear, take action and get going. As somebody told me once, you can't learn to drive a car by reading a book. You've got to get behind the wheel and practise."

"Very true words," said Frank. "How did you get on?"

"It seems obvious to me now," Simon said. "I started with the awareness stage, like you suggested. I wrote some articles talking about people's problems. I sweated blood and tears over some very detailed posts about antivirus software and do you know what happened?"

Frank was confident he did know what happened but remained quiet, inviting Simon to continue.

"Tumbleweeds! That's what happened. I had no engagement at all. Not even Susan could bring herself to like the article – and I asked her to. If this had happened in the past I would've been really frustrated and then worried and then I would've panicked. But because I was aware of my reaction, I could tell I was getting into my animal brains. Of course, I knew I had to stay in my human brain in order to come up a better solution.

"I realised I was more worried about being judged about the article than anything else. So, I asked myself the question, 'Why did this not attract attention? Why did people not show interest in this article?'. I worked out that it was because I'd used a lot of jargon. And why had I done that? Because I was trying to show I knew a lot about my subject. In other words, I was trying to impress people and trying to demonstrate my expertise. What I'd forgotten, when I went back to my notebooks, was I should've been telling stories and using clearer examples.

"I could have ditched the idea of writing on LinkedIn altogether. I could've decided, 'LinkedIn doesn't work for me'. And, the truth is, I probably would have done in the past. I would have admitted defeat and probably had another Friday night take-away banquet. This would have made me feel better, but gone nowhere. It would not have moved me forward. I would have just gone a downward spiral.

"But, by using the four quadrants and all that you showed me, I could see the way through this. So I stopped reacting and started thinking calmly. I guess you would say I went into my human brain. I went through the top row of the Thrive Framework. Not getting immediate results is not a reason to panic. It's a reason to think, learn and re-fine. I knew that my Model and Method were sound.

"So I went back to my notes and I read through what I'd written when you were telling me all about the awareness stage. You talked about regular updates and about making people aware of the consequence of the problem not just the problem itself. And that's what I did next. I started writing articles and sending messages and emails to people on a consistent basis.

"I experimented with different topics in my articles. It turns out that what business owners really wanted was to avoid a catastrophe happening. It probably helped that there was a massive ransomware attack in the news and it was suddenly on the top of people's minds. Sometimes a lucky break helps, that's for sure. I started talking about that problem and the degree of catastrophe that can happen and it was amazing to see the difference.

EARLY RESULTS

"From one of my articles, 15 people sent me messages asking for the information sheet I had compiled," Simon continued. "I'd written that information sheet following your guidance. I briefly explained the steps they needed to take to ensure their systems were safe but I didn't bombard them with details. Essentially, I was telling them how my method works, but not by describing the details. I just focused on why they needed to take these steps. Of course, I made it clear I offered that as a service."

"This sounds like really great progress Simon," said Frank. "You say 15 people contacted you. Were you happy with that number?"

"Yeah, I was delighted. I thought I needed to speak to 50 people to track down three paying clients and with 15, I was almost a third of the way there with just a few weeks in."

"What happened next?"

"Of those 15, six never got back in touch. They just took the information sheet. I followed up with them, but they didn't respond."

"How did you feel about that?"

"You won't be surprised to hear I was really hacked off. My mammalian and reptilian brains wanted to punch them in the face because that information sheet was high quality. It took me a long time to compile and it was extremely valuable to them. Honestly, I felt really frustrated they hadn't got back to me."

"Of course you felt frustrated," said Frank. "What's more, you probably felt judged. But they weren't judging you they were either judging the information sheet or they didn't really have the problem in the first place."

"You're right. I realise that now. So, that left nine of the 15. Of those, four asked a few questions, replied to my messages and then fizzled out. The conversation seemed to just run its course."

"OK. And the other five? Please don't tell me you wanted to fight with them as well," Frank chuckled.

"Here's where it gets interesting. Over the last two weeks I've met with the other five."

"Well, that's good to hear. Tell me how those meetings went."

"Ahead of the first meeting, which was my very first one of this kind, I have to say my heart was racing. This was potentially the biggest deal I could've closed with this offer, so it was a shame it happened to be my very first sales conversation in this way. I can't tell you how much I wanted to win this client."

"I can imagine," Frank empathised.

"I wanted it so much I could taste it. When I reviewed that conversation afterwards, I realised my desperation was starting to show. I forgot all about diagnosing and started telling them what I do. I had so much belief in my method. I knew I could help them, so I talked more about me than I listened to them. I guess it's not surprising they didn't take the bait. They turned me down."

"What happened as a result of that?" asked Frank.

"You'd be proud. I went to my notebook and tried to capture what I felt at the time. What I wrote was how I felt crushed. I knew that they needed help. I knew that I could help them, but they just didn't want it and I felt a huge sense of disappointment and frustration. Add in the fact this was my first one and I was genuinely concerned this wasn't going to work as a whole process."

"What happened then?"

"Well, again, I reminded myself this was an emotional response. My animal brain was back in control. I was at my wit's end. I tried to calm the animal brain by going back to that meditation recording you gave me.

THREE CONVERSION REALISATIONS

"I'll be honest; I ended up doing it on and off, not consistently like you told me to. And a fresh listen to that recording really made a difference. It helped calm the animal brain. So I calmed down and I thought it through. I looked for the clues. Why? Why didn't they buy? And I realised I'd made three big mistakes.

"The first one was that I made it more about me and less about them. It's so stupid now I think back on it, but yet it was so natural for me to do in the conversation.

"Number two was my desperation. My eagerness to get them as the client actually put them off.

"And number three was that I realised that I wasn't really listening. I was planning what to say next so I must have missed some important clues about their problem. I guess that's normal as it was my first conversation of this type, but I recognise I probably made those mistakes."

Frank's Tips 23 – For conversion success:

1) Make the conversation all about them, not about you.
2) Be unattached to the outcome to retain your power.
3) Use what they say to help them realise their own truth – that they want their problem solved and want your solution to work.

Frank looked impressed. "You may not realise it Simon, but those three realisations will change everything going forward."

"Funnily enough, it did," Simon said excitedly. "I haven't finished the story yet. For the next two businesses I met I was totally different. I was focused on them and made sure I was diagnosing their problem. So, I listened. The first of these two went like a dream. Almost before I realised what was happening, I'd signed them up as a client. As I came out of the meeting I swear I did the full fist-pump. I couldn't believe it. I walked away from that meeting high as a kite."

"This is wonderful news, congratulations," beamed Frank. "What happened then?"

"I'm a bit embarrassed to admit this. I came home and I called Susan into this kitchen. We sat at this table and I told her that this is where it all changes; this is the new way.

"She said I looked like a thing possessed and that with the next success she'd like some champagne. Sadly, the champagne wasn't needed because the next sales meeting didn't bring a new client. It turns out that when we dug into their problem that my solution wasn't right for them. They didn't need that sort of help."

"Simon, I want to congratulate you on both of those outcomes."

"On both of them? Why do you say that?"

"Well, obviously, congratulations on the first one because they signed on the dotted line. But the second one was also a great outcome because you didn't waste any time and energy trying to persuade them that you're awesome. You diagnosed the situation and concluded that they didn't have the problem that you solve and therefore they had no need for your services.

"And, importantly, you accepted that. And that freed you up to look for someone else that did have that problem and would need your help. It was very rational. It wasn't a judgement on you. That's an amazing realisation and really great practice."

"I suppose you're right. But the conversation I had with the next potential client was tricky," said Simon, remembering the event.

"Why was that?" asked Frank.

"Because they recognised that they did have the problem and they did say that they would like to work with me. But then they came back with a kicker – they wanted to negotiate on price."

"Of course they did. That was bound to happen sooner or later," acknowledge Frank. "How did you deal with that?"

"Well, do you know what? I could hardly believe what came out of my mouth. I went back to what they had said earlier in the conversation. I pointed out the impact on their business of preventing these problems. Then I reminded them of the impact on the business if these problems occurred. Then I calmly showed them the price quoted again to demonstrate it represented great value.

"I think staying calm and clear helped them agree I made a fair point. Then they agreed and signed up, too. They became my client number two."

"Simon, that's fantastic news. You were on a roll!"

"I was ecstatic," he said, beaming with self-pride. "I was starting to trust the method in my heart not just on paper. I felt that financial security was going to come much sooner than six months. Knowing what I know now, I can't believe I struggled on for so long with my own broken business model.

"The financial and relationship stress I had been going through was much worse than I'd admitted to myself. I was glad to have some hope that I could get out of this mess."

"Simon, this is like a new man speaking. You learn so amazingly well. Congratulations."

FURTHER RESULTS

Simon took the plaudits from his friend and the two men smiled. But Simon still had more of his story to tell. He held his finger up to indicate there was more to say and Frank nodded for him to continue.

"The very next business I spoke to also signed up and by then I felt like I had the Midas touch. Money was starting to flow in. And so much more easily than my previous repair offer."

"That's brilliant news, Simon. But, now I'm confused. I count three clients, but you told me you haven't made three. What do you mean?"

"One of those first contacts I thought had fizzled out came back to me. The boss, as it happened, had been away on holiday at that time and the people left in the office didn't have the authority to agree to go forward. But the boss got back to me and gave it the green light. I had written them off prematurely. I suppose, I still had a few doubts that this new business offer might not work back then. Looking back, I realise I had a belief that if they didn't keep the conversation going that they'd lost interest. I can see that was a false belief."

"Well, it seems to me you're recognising a very significant point."

"Which is?"

"That your beliefs affect the actions you end up taking."

"You're dead right," grinned Simon. "And now I have four clients signed up."

"Ha! I see. You were throwing me off the scent by saying you didn't have three clients..."

"But I didn't have three clients – I had four."

"I love it, Simon," Frank added. "This is really fantastic news."

"Wait, there's more. I have another hot prospect to see next week, so that's the last one I'm waiting on from those initial 15. The appointment is booked and that one might come in too."

"It might or it will come in?" Frank challenged him. "Beliefs Simon, beliefs."

"Well, I don't know if they've got a problem until I diagnose it, do I Frank?" Simon winked.

"Touché my friend. Congratulations."

As they laughed, they heard the front door click as Susan announced her return. She walked into the kitchen with a broad smile. "Well Frank, has he told you his news? Hasn't he done well?"

"He most certainly has," Frank replied, still smiling. "I am delighted for him. The work we covered together isn't easy. I've taken many business owners through this framework and a number of them need to have the principles explained in a few different ways before they really get it. But Simon has been an A-grade student."

SUSAN'S SIDE OF THE STORY

"The results in the business are wonderful," Frank continued. "But let's not forget that the main purpose of implementing these framework principles is not to have a better business, it's to create a life you love. If I may ask a personal question, how have your lives changed since Simon's had this new focus?"

"This coffee goes straight through you doesn't it?" Simon interjected. "I'll take this as a cue to leave you two to discuss this. Back in a minute" He hurried out of the kitchen.

It was Susan's turn to speak. "I can't thank you enough Frank. Since Simon started this business he's never seemed as certain and confident as he does now. We were both so stressed. We never had enough money coming in and I know Simon's told you our relationship was not in a good place. I know we're not out of the woods yet, but I know Simon's very confident that we will get there."

"That's great to hear," said Frank. "Has there been any impact on how you're getting on together?"

"Oh, definitely!" Susan replied enthusiastically. "He's involving me much more in what's going on with the business. Previously he kept everything so private. I'm sure he felt it was 100 per cent his responsibility. I convinced myself that he was ashamed to tell me how things were going because it would make him seem like a failure. I used to get so frustrated that he wouldn't share the pressure with me.

"But since working with you he's a different man and that has been the start of rebuilding what we've had together. In fact, only last Friday, I couldn't believe it. Normally, Friday evenings are a predictable routine of takeaway meal, sitting on the sofa with some rubbish on the TV. Within ten minutes of finishing his meal, Simon would be asleep. I usually need to prod him a couple of times for snoring. Not exactly living the dream." She smiled nervously.

Frank could see the despondency in her eyes, yet he realised there was more of the story to come.

"Well, all that was different last Friday," she went on. "Simon suggested we get a babysitter and go for a meal out." She emphasised the word 'out' as if it were a huge adventure.

"I can't remember the last time we'd eaten in a restaurant, just the two of us, without the kids. I loved it. I felt like I was getting the real Simon back. It's been a long, slow decline. I hated seeing him working himself so hard and struggling so much. And I hated being powerless to help him. He kept saying it would all work out, but I'm not sure if he was telling me or trying to convince himself.

"But the meal out last Friday meant so much. And if that was a pleasant surprise, he then went one step further."

Frank paused, unsure of where the conversation was headed. But Susan smiled and shook her head. "He suggested we repaint the lounge," she said with a laugh. "I've been talking about it for ages and he said he felt it could do with freshening up, too, and wanted to make it seem newer. What's more, he suggested we paint it together! He'd never have had the time or energy to even think about such an idea until now."

"Honestly Frank, I'm not sure what kind of magic spell you've cast, but you have genuinely given Simon a new lease of life. He has the energy to spend time with the kids again. And it struck me the other day that I was aware of the sound of laughter in the house. I hadn't realised it, but this has been missing for far too long. I am so grateful! Thank you."

"Thank you Susan. I appreciate those kind words, but I have to say it's not magic and it's not about me. It's the way Simon has committed to this process that is making such a positive difference. He now understands how he can serve the best clients for his business. He's redesigned how to do that through his own Method. This creates financial security, which is now only a few months away.

ALL 3FS

"More than that, it sounds like he's taken on board the importance of the 3Fs. He's realised that making money the entire focus makes the situation worse for what actually matters most in life – your relationship together, having a happy and safe family with the kids, and experiencing trips out like you did last Friday. These all create fun and fulfilling lives.

"Most of the work Simon and I have done together so far has been to get the first F in place; financial security. What you're saying tells me he's already working on his ECG too."

"Working on his ECG? Does he have a heart problem?" asked Susan, her face revealing some concern.

"Ah, no," he reassured her. "ECG is a mnemonic I use in the framework I've shown Simon. I'll leave it to him to explain it to you. But the point is that life is for living and not for working yourself into the ground."

"We have really turned the corner," she sighed. "His work is picking up and already we're getting on so much better."

Simon strolled back into the kitchen with a smile on his face. "I think my ears are burning," he said.

"They should be," Frank replied. "And it's all very encouraging."

"Things are going much better now for sure," Simon said, putting an arm around his wife. "I can see that if I keep going we're certainly going to have financial security in a few months from now. I do have the stomach to tackle what's needed. I'm no longer so burned out and defeated. I can see growth happening. The first F, financial security, is going to arrive. I love the feeling. I can almost smell it.

"But Frank, I don't want to stop there. Once I've got financial security, which is not far away now, I want the second F as well. I want to create freedom. All six freedoms you told me about!"

Frank smiled, knowingly. "Wonderful Simon! I'd be delighted to show you how to get those. First, though, you know you had gaps in your knowledge and skills for financial security? You won't be surprised to learn you have gaps about how to achieve freedom, as well.

"We'll need to cover principles for building, developing and growing a team. Principles for creating systems so you can stop being self-employed and become a business owner."

"I thought I was already a business owner?" Simon was curious.

"You're on your way," Frank assured him. "What you call your business can certainly give you financial security. But to have the second F – freedom – you'll need to make it work in a very different way. Don't worry; everything you're doing right now is exactly the right thing to be doing. You must have financial security first. You cannot have the freedoms without financial security. That's why I described it as like putting on your own oxygen mask first."

"I've got a whole lot more to learn. Is that what you're saying?" Simon's voice sounded a little deflated.

"You have and isn't that great?" Frank added. "We use the same framework, the same four quadrants and the same 12 principles, but we just take each one to a deeper level. From everything I've seen, I know you'll do well on the second stage of your 3Fs journey."

"Well, thanks for the encouragement. I can certainly feel my self-belief coming back. Can we start the next stage now?"

FIRST THINGS FIRST

Frank's reply wiped the smile from Simon's face.

"I'm afraid not. It would be the wrong thing to do at this stage. As I mentioned just now, freedom needs financial security in place. You're not quite there yet. You are heading firmly towards your financial security. You know exactly how much you need and you know exactly how to get there.

"You're ahead of your own schedule with such great progress winning new clients. Beyond winning more clients, remember, you still need to deliver your service. And the purpose of delivery is?" He was testing Simon.

"To retain clients," Simon recalled.

"Right! If your delivery was below your promise then you'd be chasing new clients all the time and you wouldn't have financial security. You certainly couldn't build a business to give you freedom if that was the situation.

"So, first things first. Let's make sure you do what's needed to ensure you have financial security. Let's get that firmly in place first and then we can put the next pieces of the puzzle in place so that you get the second F of freedom."

Although disappointed not to be moving on again, Simon could see why Frank's life worked so well – he didn't get distracted by the next goal. He stayed focused and kept things simple. It was true. Simon didn't yet have financial security. He was certainly building momentum and he was treating this as enough. Frank's advice was, yet again, exactly what he needed to hear.

"I really look forward to getting together again and hearing when you've got financial security and I'm totally there for you to support you in the next stage," Frank told his friend.

"One more thing: You will get stuck as you grow to financial security. It's inevitable. It's not a weakness or a fault; it's a necessary part of growth."

"I already have been stuck," agreed Simon. "It took me quite a while to find a way through the problems."

"In which case, Simon, I invite you to be a bit smarter next time. Yes, you have the capability to work things out on your own. But, remember the TME resources? By working through problems on your own, you're allocating your time and energy resources. Consequently, you're likely to be taking longer than you need to solve your problems. This will also deplete your energy reserves. There's also the risk you won't come up with an effective solution."

"You're suggesting I ask for help in those situations?" Simon asked.

"Not only am I suggesting you do," said Frank. "I'm inviting you to ask me. As I came here today, I was very aware you hadn't asked me for any help in the last two months. I'll be honest, when other people I've worked with go into their own bunker like you did, they have struggled to make progress.

"It's hard to work things out on your own. But not only is it hard, it's also not very smart. It's slower and it's risky. I'm inviting you to avoid those risks and mistakes. You have a resource here. It's only you who can choose to use it."

Frank's Tips 24 – Trying to work things out on your own is a longer and riskier approach than you need. Find a mentor. Use them. Build clarity. Build momentum.

"Frank, thank you so much," Simon's gratitude was clear and sincere.

"Thank you from me, too," added Susan. "This is truly wonderful. What you've taught Simon already has done more than create the way to have financial security. If the truth be told, you've also saved our marriage."

"That's very kind, Susan," said Frank. "I'm not sure I'm ready to be a marriage guidance counsellor, but I'm really glad that things are going so well for you guys now. Your support is so important for Simon and long may that continue."

"Thanks again, Frank, for all your help so far," Simon said. "I'm going to come back to you in a couple months to report back. By then I'll make sure we've achieved financial security. Then we can dive straight into the freedom."

"Simon, you are an amazing learner and you take action. I really look forward to that. Get in touch sooner if you're stuck – do not stay stuck. Good luck over the next two months."

As Simon closed the front door behind Frank, he turned to Susan and they hugged each other. It was a long, deep and loving hug.

He knew Susan believed in him. What's more, he believed in himself. When he left his last job, he jumped into self-employment. He could see now how naïve he'd been. It was inevitable that he would struggle as much as he had. He was a skilful tech guy, but his corporate wage-slave days had done nothing to prepare him for self-employment. This was a completely different game. It was a game he didn't know the rules for.

But now Frank had shown him.

In the next two months, if all went to plan, he and Susan would have financial security. This was an incredible turnaround from the depths he'd experienced.

But in truth, he could already see financial security as achieved. His method was working. He'd proved it. He couldn't help but imagine what the business would look like if he'd achieved freedom – working when he wanted to and having staff to deliver the service, look after the finances and win new clients.

This new possibility excited him. He felt that he'd served his time working for a big company and definitely served his time as a struggling self-employed person. He deserved more. Susan deserved more. Their kids certainly deserved more.

Yes, freedom would be his focus.

As they let go of each other, he looked into Susan's eyes. He smiled. She sensed an air of certainty in him.

He said two words: "It's time."

APPENDIX – THE THRIVE FRAMEWORK AND ALL 3FS

The Thrive Framework contains all 12 principles to design a smarter business for a better life.

There are two columns – "personal" and "business". You cannot create a successful business without personal development work. The main problem faced by most small businesses is the owner and not the business itself. The Framework ties both columns together, each feeding the other in an interdependent dynamic.

The Framework also has two rows – "internal" and "external". The external row represents what the world sees; what is happening "external to your head". The internal row represents the opportunity to think before acting; to be "internal to your head". Mindful action will produce best external performance.

The Thrive Framework can be described in a clockwise story starting with the Reason quadrant (personal, external), and working through the other quadrants of Self and Resources to arrive at Momentum where the business performance will deliver what's been defined by the 3Fs in the Reason quadrant. Begin with the end in mind, as some wise author once advised.

Figure 16: The complete Thrive Framework

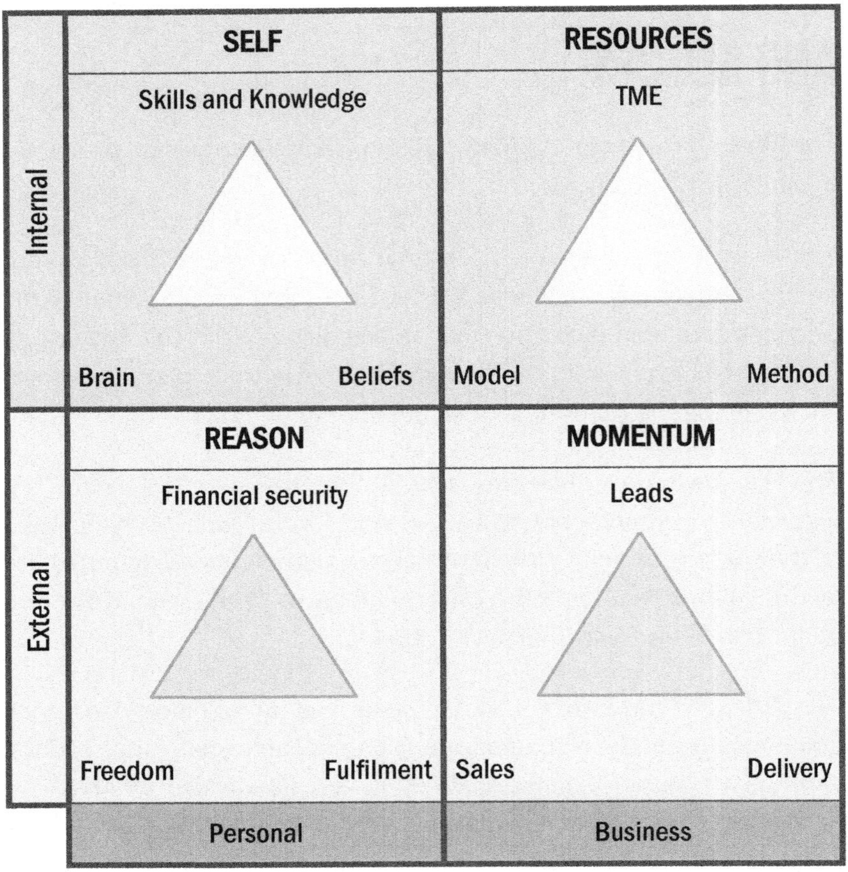

	SELF	RESOURCES
Internal	Skills and Knowledge Brain · · · · · Beliefs	TME Model · · · · · Method
External	REASON Financial security Freedom · · · · · Fulfilment	MOMENTUM Leads Sales · · · · · Delivery
	Personal	Business

Figure 17: Reason quadrant described

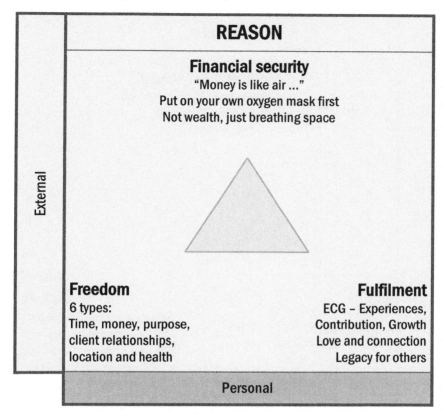

The purpose of your business is not to keep you busy. When you're working too hard – with or without great results – you're suffering from The Busyness Delusion.

The purpose of your business is to provide you with all 3Fs: Financial security, Freedom and Fulfilment.

Freedom is more than, 'I can take a day off if I wish.'

Fulfilment is more than, 'I quite enjoy my work.'

Figure 18: Self quadrant described

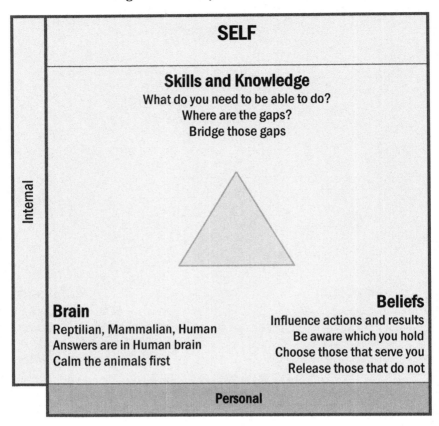

Your brain's primary job is to keep you safe. It perceives threat when you risk being judged. It triggers emotional reactions, including fear, anger and aggrieved righteousness. Such emotions prevent creative thinking and problem solving.

It's normal to have unconscious and unquestioned beliefs about a situation. Often such beliefs do not serve you and hold you back. Examine the evidence to choose beliefs to serve you.

Skills and knowledge gaps are inevitable, but can be bridged.

Figure 19: Resources quadrant described

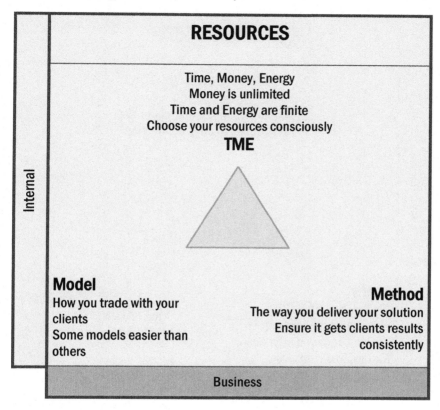

Your access to money is limited only by your thinking. Choosing to build your business from scarce and finite resources can be slower or riskier than from using unlimited resources.

Design a Model to create your 3Fs as easily as possible. Charging by the hour or day is one of the hardest options available.

Ensure your solution delivers results to your clients consistently.

Figure 20: Momentum quadrant described

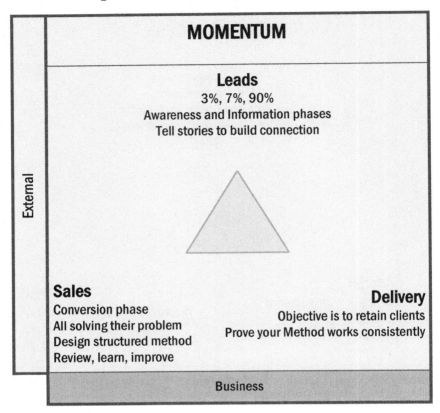

Competition is toughest when fighting for the attention of the smallest minority of your potential market.

Understand how the AIC approach opens up 90 per cent of the market where there is very little competition. Design and implement messages and campaigns to attract the 90 per cent and then deliver your solution to retain them as future clients.

BIBLIOGRAPHY/RECOMMENDED READING

Masterson, Michael. *Ready, Fire, Aim: Zero to $100 Million in No Time Flat*, Hoboken, New Jersey: John Wiley & Sons, Inc., 2008.

Warrillow, John. *Built to Sell: Creating a Business That Can Thrive Without You*, London: Penguin Books Ltd., 2011.

Harris, Dan. *10% Happier: How I Tamed the Voice in My Head, Reduced Stress Without Losing My Edge, and Found Self-Help That Actually Works - A True Story*, London: Hodder & Stoughton Ltd., 2014.

Cialdini PhD, Robert B. *Influence: The Psychology of Persuasion*, New York: HarperCollins e-books, 2009.

Eagleman, David. *Incognito: The Secret Lives of the Brain*, Edinburgh: Canongate Books Ltd., 2011.

Silver, Yanik. *Evolved Enterprise: An Illustrated Guide to Re-Think, Re-Imagine & Re-Invent Your Business to Deliver Meaningful Impact & Even Greater Profits*, Washington, DC: Ideapress Publishing, 2017.

Keller, Gary. *The One Thing: The Surprisingly Simple Truth Behind Extraordinary Results*, London: Hodder & Stoughton Ltd., 2013.

Newport, Cal. *Deep Work: Rules for Focused Success in a Distracted World*, London: Piatkus, 2016.

Jiwa, Bernadette. *Meaningful: The Story of Ideas That Fly*, Australia: Perceptive Press, 2015.

Hanson, Rick. *Buddha's Brain: The Practical Neuroscience of Happiness, Love & Wisdom*, Oakland: New Harbinger Publications, Inc., 2009.

Covey, Stephen R. *The 7 Habits of Highly Effective People*, New York: RosettaBooks LLC, 2013 (electronic edition)

RESOURCES

Frank provides Simon with various resources during their time together. As a reader of this book, you have access to the same resources.

CHAPTER 1 (THE REASON):

Self-assessment test: Find where you are on the 3Fs spectrum

The starting point on any journey is to work out where you are now and where you want to get to. This self-assessment tool is available at thebusynessdelusion.com for you to use as soon as you are ready.

CHAPTER 2 (HEAD INSIDE):

Meditation recording

Simon was reticent to try meditation as it was new to him and he was unsure how to go about it. Frank gave him a recording to guide him so he could find out how easy and energising it can be.

This guided meditation recording is available to you to stream or download at thebusynessdelusion.com

CHAPTER 3 (SMARTER, NOT HARDER):

Model maths: Spreadsheet tool

Frank explained to Simon that charging by the hour is one of the hardest models to choose. By using columns in his notebook, Simon could work out how many clients he would need at different prices in order to achieve his own financial security.

You don't need to work it out in a notebook because a spreadsheet tool is available that allows you to see the financial effect of changing just three variables – how many clients to add each month, the price you'll charge and how long they'll stay with you.

Don't be surprised if your own financial security is much easier than you thought. The spreadsheet is available at: thebusynessdelusion.com

KEEP IN TOUCH

I hope you've been inspired and recognise the insights Frank shared with Simon. You can take the 12 principles in this book and put them into practice in your own business.

I'd love to know the effect when you do. My purpose is to help 1,000 business owners create a 3Fs business and life so they can create their own legacy – their own impact in the world. I invite you to contact me to let me know how you've implemented the principles and what results you've experienced.

Please get in touch via the website:
http://thebusynessdelusion.com.

As you've seen from Simon, you get results much more easily and quickly with the support of the right mentor. Below are some of the ways I can be the right mentor for you. I invite you to explore with an open mind and find the right solution for your personal situation. I look forward to hearing from you.

You can find the following offers at thebusynessdelusion.com too.

FINANCIAL SECURITY PROGRAMME (FSP)

A 12-month implementation programme with full mentor support. The promise: You will achieve your financial security in six to 12 months and in the unlikely event you haven't reached it after 12 months (but you will!) we'll continue to support you for free until you do. In other words, everyone who joins the FSP will leave with financial security on their terms.

FREEDOM PROGRAMME

A 12-month implementation programme to create the six freedoms. With financial security already in place (via the FSP if necessary), the priority is then to transform your business to give you time freedom via a teachable and repeatable method. With time freedom established, we then implement the method to achieve the other five freedoms in sequence.

FULFILMENT PROGRAMME

With financial security and freedom now established, the focus moves to living with Fulfilment. This is an ongoing mentor-support programme to transform personal life and create a legacy. Using our ECG framework, we guide you to create a life previously unimaginable; with loving relationships, inspiring adventures, beautiful environments, high personal growth and meaningful contribution. You also have the opportunity to be involved with the Gift of a Future movement to create your own impact in the world, proving this is the most special and amazing time to be alive.

PERSONAL MENTORING AND COACHING

Chris works with a maximum of six one-to-one clients per year. Each client commits to designing an extraordinary life free from limiting beliefs and inspired by a personal purpose.

Likely covering every area of life, the aim is to create a future more attractive than its past. The objective for each client is transformation. The distinction is that change is temporary and transformation is permanent. Life is more attractive when you're pulled towards a compelling future.

Printed in Great Britain
by Amazon